a Consumer Publication

HOW TO SUE
IN THE
COUNTY COURT

Consumers' Association
publishers of **Which?**
14 Buckingham Street
London WC2N 6DS

a Consumer Publication

edited by Edith Rudinger

published by Consumers' Association
publishers of **Which?**

Consumer Publications are
available from Consumers'
Association and from
booksellers. Details of other
Consumer Publications are
given at the end of this book.

©Consumers' Association, October 1973
reprinted January 1974
amended reprint September 1975
ISBN 0 85202 105 4

Computer typeset
and printed offset litho
by Page Bros (Norwich) Ltd.

CONTENTS

Foreword

Courts and legal rights   *page* 1

Letters before action   10

Suing   28

Preparing for battle   66

Pre-trial review and after   93

The hearing   154

Being sued   216

After the hearing   229

Index   240

FOREWORD

It is all very well telling you that you are entitled to claim your money back if something you bought turns out to be defective. But this advice is not much good if the seller refuses to pay, and you are unable to bring a court action to get it because you fear the expense of going to law or do not know what is involved in attempting to take a case to court without a solicitor.

This book enables you to sue in the county court, without a solicitor, in a consumer case. It takes you step by step through what is involved in bringing a case, and explains the procedures and rules.

Many cases are settled well before the trial, some soon after the summons is issued and served. The chances are, therefore, that you will not have to take your case beyond the stage described in the first three chapters of the book. If, however, yours turns out to be one of the few cases which does end up with a trial, this book explains what you will have to do all the way through. It describes a comparatively difficult case, involving some technicalities. With a bit of luck, your case could be much simpler.

Solicitors do not face ruin with the publication of this book. On the contrary, they will probably welcome it. Small consumer claims in the county court are generally a nuisance to most solicitors, time-consuming and uneconomic. You may well, therefore, be doing your solicitor a kindness if, instead of troubling him to act for you in pursuing a consumer complaint in the county court, you do it yourself. You will also, of course, be saving the fees you would have to pay him if he acted for you.

For many years the county court has been the preserve of lawyers and debt collectors. That is now changing. The government has accepted the necessity of making the county court more accessible to consumers as a means of obtaining redress. Since October 1973 a new arbitration service has been in operation in the county court, so that the procedure can be even simpler.

This book covers cases in England and Wales only. The scottish legal system is quite different, and that in Northern Ireland is somewhat different again.

The main stages of suing in the county court on a consumer's claim

1	letter before action, making a formal claim	consumer to shop
2	letter repudiating liability	shop to consumer
3	find out address of registered office of shop	consumer from Companies' House
4	prepare particulars of claim	consumer
5	issue county court summons	consumer (plaintiff) at court office
6	service of summons	court on shop (defendant)
7	(optional) request for further and better particulars	defendant to plaintiff
8	prepare defence	defendant
9	defence filed at court	defendant
10	defence sent to consumer	court to plaintiff
11	pre-trial review	plaintiff and defendant

either

12	arbitration	plaintiff defendant registrar

or, if no arbitration

12	preparation of list of documents (form C.C.83A)	plaintiff and defendant
13	inspection of documents	plaintiff and defendant
14	complete and serve notice to admit (C.C.119)	defendant to plaintiff and plaintiff to defendant
15	complete and serve notice to produce (C.C.120)	defendant to plaintiff and plaintiff to defendant
16	prepare copies of documents needed at trial and put into logical bundles if necessary	plaintiff and defendant
17	issue and serve witness summonses	plaintiff to his witnesses defendant to his witnesses
18	swear and file affidavit of service of witness summonses (form 116/2) where applicable	plaintiff at court defendant at court
19	trial	plaintiff, defendant, witnesses
20	judgment sent	court to loser
21	taxation of costs (where applicable)	winner to court and loser
22	enforcement of judgment (where applicable)	winner (and court) to loser

STOP PRESS: *page 62*

As this edition went to press, county court fees were again increased and are now as follows for issuing a summons:

	amount claimed	court fee £
not exceeding	£10	1.00
over	£10 to £15	2.50
"	£15 to £20	3.00
"	£20 to £30	4.00
"	£30 to £50	5.00
"	£50 to £80	6.00
"	£80 to £100	7.00
"	£100 to £200	8.00
"	£200 to £500	10.00
"	£500	12.00

In addition, bailiff's fees for service of summons (page 64) are now between £1 and £2, depending on the amount of the claim. Also, the fees to obtain a warrant of execution (page 235) have been altered.

There are four court systems in England and Wales, two criminal, and two civil. Serious criminal cases are dealt with in crown courts (formerly known as quarter sessions and assizes), the best known of which is the Old Bailey, officially called the Central Criminal Court, in London. Minor criminal cases are dealt with in magistrates courts, sometimes still called (quite wrongly) police courts.

Serious civil cases, such as claims for heavy damages for personal injury, libel and slander cases, and disputes between large companies about commercial matters, are dealt with in the High Court, which is divided into three divisions: the Queen's Bench Division, the Chancery Division and the Family Division. Minor civil cases (those where not more than £1000 is at stake) are dealt with in county courts, of which there are over 300 in England and Wales. There is a local county court for every district in the country, not just one for each county, and generally a case is brought in the court for the locality where the facts happened. This book describes what happens in a case brought in a county court.

A judge decides a court case on its facts and the law. However sympathetic he may feel to a person who has apparently suffered a wrong, the judge must apply the law as he finds it. You will not win a case just because it would be ridiculous or very hard for you to lose. Not every complaint is suitable for taking to court; claims inspired by moral indignation, the desire to air a grievance, or a campaign to reform something, are not.

You will only win if there has been an infringement

of a legal right. Imagine that a shop refused to sell you a particular article, without explaining why. You would be understandably angry at this, so much so that you may think of taking the matter to court. There would be no point in doing so, because you have no legal right to be sold any particular article displayed in a shop. But if a shop were to give you short measure, even by a small amount and entirely by accident, you could claim for the loss, and your claim would be upheld in court. This is because you have a legal right to receive the amount you ask for.

—questions of fact

A court case may be contested on its facts, its law or both. If the facts are disputed, one side says that so-and-so happened, while the other says it happened differently. To decide who wins, the court must consider the evidence and decide what in fact happened. A witness may be lying, or his memory may be at fault. Of some facts there may be no direct evidence at all, so that it is necessary to draw inferences in order to decide what happened. Court procedure is designed to find out facts as effectively as possible. Each witness is first asked questions by the side which called him. This is examination-in-chief. He is then open to questioning by the opposite side: cross-examination. A lawyer's skill can make a tremendous difference to the examination of witnesses. If facts are contested, especially if witnesses may be lying, the skill of an advocate is worth hiring.

—questions of law

Sometimes, argument centres on the law to be applied to the case. One side says that, accepting that the facts are so-and-so, the law gives a result in his favour. In support of the argument, he may refer to acts of parliament, legal text books and previously decided court cases. The other side contends for a different interpretation, by corresponding argument. Legal argument like this can only be presented adequately by a lawyer with a thorough understanding of what it is all about and text books and law reports on previous cases. If, therefore, a case involves a serious issue of law, it is not one to be taken by a layman, even if he has a general understanding of the law.

without a solicitor

If it is sensible to employ a lawyer in a case where there is a dispute about the facts or about the law, what cases are left where a lawyer may not be needed? There are certainly some. Suppose that you have complained to a shop about a faulty appliance, but without effect. Your complaint may have been rebuffed out of elementary ignorance on the part of the shop. They do not dispute that you bought the appliance there, nor that your appliance no longer works. They suggest that you go to the manufacturer, and refer to the guarantee. They say that they are unable to accept responsibility. But by law it is the shop's responsibility. In such a case there is no real dispute about the facts or the law; both are on your side. Yet in order to pursue your complaint you have to take the case to court, or at least threaten to do so.

As another example, imagine that your car has been damaged in a road accident which was entirely and unquestionably the fault of the other driver. On no possible view was the accident your fault, and you are anxious not to involve your own insurance company, for fear of putting in jeopardy your no-claims bonus. Or you may have been paid by your insurance company for the cost of repairing your own car, but now wish to be paid by the other driver for the cost of hiring another car while yours was off the road, and for a refund of the excess on your policy, that is, the proportion of the claim on your policy which you have to pay out of your own pocket.

These are claims which it is sometimes possible for a layman to take to court without instructing a solicitor. In both, common sense probably tells him that he has a good claim which would very likely be upheld by a judge. And both are based on legal rights which have been infringed.

In the case of the claim against the shop, the legal right arose from a contract. In buying the appliance, the consumer made a contract of sale with the proprietor of the shop. The gist of the contract was that, in exchange for paying the price, the buyer became the owner of the article. Some of the terms of the contract were specifically agreed: the price and what was to be bought. Other terms of the contract were implied by law: terms about the quality of the article, and its fitness for the purpose for which it was to be used. These terms are implied by the Sale of Goods Act 1893. If therefore a consumer finds that something new he has recently bought does not work properly, he has a good claim for the cost of putting it right. If the defect is substantial, so that an average person knowing about it would not even have bought the article in the first place, the buyer can cancel the purchase, and claim all his money back, provided he acts promptly. He will, of course, have to return the article. The point is this: the claim for the cost of repair, or to have your money back, is backed up by a legal right, a right derived from the contract, and implied by the Sale of Goods Act.

In the case of the claim against the other driver involved in an accident, there is no question of a contract. You cannot claim against the other man's insurance company because you had no contract with them. Your claim lies against the other driver involved, under the law of negligence. A person is liable to compensate the victims of his negligence. Put simply, it is a question of deciding whose fault it was. The cost of repairing a damaged car, compensation for personal injuries, and the reimbursement of out-of-pocket expences (such as hiring another car during the repair of your own), can all be claimed against the person responsible. They all form part of a claim for damages for negligence.

Another case which could be handled without a solicitor is a straightforward claim for the recovery of a debt. If, for example, you sold your car privately, and the buyer did not pay what was owing for the price, you could sue him for this yourself. Or if you were prevailed upon to make a loan and the borrower failed to repay, you could take the matter to court yourself.

hire purchase

A sphere where court actions abound is hire purchase and other forms of buying on credit. The commonest situation is where a person buying goods on hire purchase is sued by the finance company for outstanding instalments. It is normal for the initiative to be taken by the finance company. If there is a dispute, often the question is how much money the consumer must pay to clear his debt with the finance company. If the consumer pays what he thinks is due, the finance company must either accept the payment or take the matter to court. The consumer need do nothing—he can wait for the court summons to arrive. (Sometimes it does not.) Although the initial action has to be taken by the finance company, the outcome of the case still depends on the consumer's legal rights. If the finance company has a legal right to the money, it will win its case. If you have a legal right to withhold payment, you will win.

being sued

It is not only in hire purchase cases that the consumer may be the one taken to court, rather than the one who takes the case there. The consumer is sometimes in a position to put the burden of testing the matter in court on to the firm with which he has a dispute. Suppose you order coal, and delivery within a week is promised, since you made clear at the time of the order the importance of prompt delivery. Suppose then that the delivery is not made until three weeks have passed. In this case, the suppliers are in breach of their contract with you. You made it a term of the contract that the coal would be delivered in one week; they broke that term. Here you have a right to receive damages for breach of the contract. The amount of your damages is likely to be disputed; it is the amount which would reasonably compensate you for being without the fuel for two weeks. A fair figure for this, in the depths of winter, might be £3. You would be entitled to deduct £3 from the coal bill. This would probably produce an explosive response. Never mind, you are acting within your legal rights. If the supplier wishes to dispute your legal right to do this, or the amount of your deduction, he must sue you for what he regards as the amount outstanding on his bill. You would then defend the case, maintaining that you owe nothing, because the amount owed to you for damages for late delivery has been set against the amount due on the bill. In a case like this, it would be up to the supplier to take the initiative by bringing the court action. If the case ended up in court, it would be for you to prove your right to damages for late delivery.

It is impossible to give a definitive list of the kinds of court action which a layman could bring without being represented by a solicitor. People differ: one person might win a court action which another would not even attempt. The procedure to be followed will be illustrated by reference to an action which is quite likely to be brought by the would-be litigant in person: a claim against a shop in connection with a faulty appliance.

To be involved in a court case is seldom a pleasure, and often both sides are dissatisfied with the result. Litigation is inclined to be uncertain, expensive, frustrating and time-consuming. Two hazards in particular stand out: costs and enforcement.

costs and enforcement
The loser in a county court case is generally ordered to pay the legal costs of the winner. What he has to pay varies according to the amount at stake. The amount which the winner receives from the loser hardly ever covers all his legal expenses, particularly if he instructs a solicitor. As a result, the fruits of his victory are usually reduced to meet further legal expenses. To launch a case in court puts at risk not only the amount for which you sue: if you lose, you will have to pay your own legal costs and the other side's costs as well. These costs could amount to far more than the amount of your claim. Many an enthusiastic litigant, certain of triumph in the temple of justice, has ended up in misery paying off legal costs by instalments.

Even if you obtain judgment in your favour, you may run into difficulty in enforcing it. Yours may prove to be a hollow victory. If you win your case, and your opponent is ordered to pay you, say, £50, he still may not pay you. There are official ways of enforcing a judgment against a man, including selling up his furniture, diversion of part of his earnings or his bank account, making him pay by instalments, or making him bankrupt. But if he simply has not got the money, or has disappeared, your court judgment is nothing but a piece of paper. Be sure, then, that your opponent is not what lawyers call a man of straw—entirely without the means to pay—before starting your case against him.

Lastly, do you have the patience and the determination that may be needed to see a court case through to its end? It may take months, even years, before the whole business is disposed of. By the time you get into court, the anger originally felt for your adversary, which drove you to launch the case, may have been transferred to the system of justice as administered in the county court. If you get bogged down in abstruse procedural questions, or the other side causes delays and difficulties before the matter gets anywhere near being tried in court, you may curse the day you ever heard of the county court, or bought this book. You may then be able to back out of the case only if you pay the other side's costs so far. Only if you are quite sure that you will persevere to the end, should you start a court case—or even contemplate starting one.

Emma Seaton is not quarrelsome by nature. Neither is her husband Matthew. But when their quite new washing machine stopped working in the middle of an extra large wash, though not before it had pumped a quantity of water over the floor of the kitchen, they felt that the time had come for action.

Emma telephoned the service department of the manufacturer first thing next morning, explained what had happened, and stressed the urgency. The service department expressed the hope of coming 'in a day or two, but we cannot promise'. The situation did not encourage optimism. From previous experience, the delay could be more than a week.

Matthew and Emma were pretty fed up with their washing machine. Emma had bought it seven months previously at a local department store. It was a brand Emma had never heard of before, but the price looked reasonable and its appearance was impressive. The manufacturer's written guarantee said that defects in manufacture would be corrected free of charge for 12 months, and the manufacturer's own service department was responsible for doing this. Within a week of buying the machine, the Seatons had trouble with it, and there had since been two further occasions on which the machine had required attention. Each time there had been delay before the mechanic arrived. During these periods of breakdown, Emma had been forced to take the family washing to the launderette, and it looked as if this was going to be the routine on this occasion too.

Emma made a note of what she was spending at the launderette while the washing machine was out of use. This would be claimed, if they ever reached the stage of making a formal complaint. For the present, they decided, they would do no more than prepare the ground for doing so.

Their claim legally would be against the store—Watsons—where Emma had bought the machine. Although the guarantee was provided by the manufacturer—Toltons Domestic Appliances Ltd—it was against the seller that they would look for redress, from the legal point of view.

Matthew and Emma decided to allow seven days for the machine to be put right, before taking the next step. If it was not operating normally by then, they would cancel the purchase, and claim compensation from the shop. For the time being, nothing further had to be done.

After four days, Emma again telephoned the service department of the manufacturer to find out what was happening. She was told that the mechanic had it on his list, but he was rather busy, and it was not known when he would be calling on them.

The seven days went by and the mechanic still had not come. The time for action had arrived. Action consisted in the first instance of writing two letters. The first was to the shop where the washing machine had been bought. Emma was the one who had ordered it, so it was she who had to write the letters; it makes no difference who paid for it. If the machine were on hire purchase, the same procedure would be adopted, except that a corresponding letter would be written to the finance company, who is legally responsible, at the same time informing the shop.

Emma sensibly kept a copy of her letter, as she

did of all the correspondence that followed. Her letter
to the shop—Watsons—was as follows:

14 Twintree Avenue,
Minford, Surrey.
11 December 1972.

Dear Sirs,

*I bought a Washfaster washing machine (model number
DB 8732/67G) from you seven months ago at the price of
£84.50. The guarantee says that defects in the machine are
dealt with by the manufacturer's service department. For
this reason, I have so far been in touch with them (Toltons
Domestic Appliances Ltd) on the several occasions when
the machine has broken down. Neither the machine itself,
nor the attention given to it by Toltons, has proved at all
satisfactory.*

*Within a week of your having installed it, the machine
stopped completely, and it was over two weeks before Toltons' mechanic arrived to put it right. Since then, there
have been two further occasions when the machine has
required attention. On one of these, it was again a fort-
night before the mechanic came to repair it. He was then
unable to do so, and there was a further delay before I
could use it once more.*

*Now the machine has broken down yet again and has
been out of use for a week. As before, I got in touch with
Toltons, but so far their mechanic has not come here to put
it right.*

*The frequency and the completeness of the breakdowns
demonstrate that the machine is not capable of performing
reliably. I have given the manufacturer a fair opportunity
of putting it right on the several occasions I mentioned.*

*I therefore cancel my purchase from you, and require
you to remove what is now your machine from my house
and to refund the price I paid you for it, namely £84.50.*

*Please collect the machine and refund the price within
seven days. I also propose to claim from you the additional
expense I have incurred through having a faulty machine.*

*I am writing to Toltons telling them what I have said to
you, making clear that I will not at present allow the
machine to be repaired by their mechanic, in case it is later
needed as evidence in support of my case.*

Yours faithfully,

Emma Seaton

Messrs. Watsons Stores (Minford) Ltd,
12 High Street,
Minford, Surrey.

cancelling a contract

A buyer's right to cancel a contract in this way
depends on the terms of the purchase. Only if the
purchase contract itself so provides, can the buyer
cancel it. Usually there is no written contract, no
explicitly agreed terms at all. The buyer's rights are
governed by the Sale of Goods Act 1893, which says
that if the goods are not fit for their intended purpose,
or are not of merchantable quality, or are not as
described, the buyer may cancel the deal. An article
is unmerchantable if a reasonable person would not
buy it knowing what it is really like, what defects it
has, and how it will turn out. The legal requirements
that an article should, when sold, be fit for its
intended purpose, be of merchantable quality, and
comply with its description are basic terms of a contract for the sale of goods; so basic, in fact, that if
any one of them is broken, the buyer, when he discovers
it, can call the whole thing off.

—cancelling in time

It was necessary for Emma to act promptly in exercising her right of cancellation. She had given the manufacturer a chance, on three earlier occasions, to put the machine right. Now they had a final opportunity, but had not taken it. As soon as that opportunity had passed, Emma wrote to cancel the contract, so that she could not be accused of delay. It is not always easy to know what amounts to delay. If the buyer is too late in cancelling the purchase, all is not lost, however: he is entitled to compensation for getting a faulty article. This amounts to the difference between the price paid and the value of the faulty article (which remains his property). Because it is difficult after the first few weeks to be sure whether your cancellation is in time, it is best to assume that you are in time, and cancel. When it comes to making a claim you then claim a refund of the price, based on the assumption that the cancellation was in time and, as an alternative to it, claim damages for up to the same amount, in case your cancellation was too late.

In some cases, the passing of a few hours, even minutes, could well be too late. That would be the case, for example, with a choc-ice bought from a stall on the seafront. It is no good coming back after a few minutes and complaining that it was partly melted when you bought it. The time to complain about that was there and then, when you bought it. In such a case, the passing of even a few minutes makes a cancellation of purchase too late. Put legally, you accepted the choc-ice in that you failed to tell the seller that you rejected it before the expiry of a reasonable time—a reasonable time in those circumstances being something less than three minutes. On the other hand, it could well be that a housewife buys a carton of choc-ices, takes it straight home, puts it in the freezer, and only takes it out after, say, 18 months. When the carton is opened and one of the choc-ices is unwrapped and bitten into, there is a dead spider in the middle of it. Quite apart from any interest that the local health department might take in the case, the housewife can reject the purchase, that is cancel it, although she has had that carton of choc-ices for 18 months. It is only when she gets it out of the freezer and opens one of the bars that she discovers that there is a fault in it. Only then does she discover that she has reason to reject it. In that case, the reasonable period carries on until the moment of realisation arrives. From then on she must act promptly, of course. But provided she does, she is not too late.

The right to rescind a contract, if a basic term is broken, carries with it the right to have the price refunded in full. It is not necessary to give credit for the value of having had some use out of the article in the period before the purchase is cancelled. In addition, the buyer may claim compensation for any expenses directly and predictably incurred by reason of the article being defective. In this case, for instance, Emma would be entitled to be refunded the extra cost of having her washing done in the launderette, while her own washing machine was useless. And this would not be confined to the expenses during the breakdown immediately preceding the cancellation—the expenses arising from the earlier breakdowns could be claimed as well. With an eye to the possibility that there would be an argument about the cause of the trouble, Emma suggested that the machine should not be further tinkered with, at least not until both sides had agreed what the cause of the trouble was. In effect, Emma was notifying the shop that she did not wish the evidence supporting her claim to be touched.

letter before action

Emma's letter was, in effect, what solicitors call a letter before action. This is a formal notification of a claim. It need not be phrased in a legalistic way, nor need technical legal words be used. An intelligent letter before action can result in the claim being met satisfactorily without more ado. Obviously, if it is written by, and on the headed notepaper of, a firm of solicitors, it is likely to be taken more seriously by the person who receives it. This is what gives a solicitor's letter an extra something. But there is very little which can be said in a solicitor's letter before action which cannot be said in one written by a layman who knows what to say.

In the passion of putting forward a claim, it is easy to forget that your letter may one day be looked at most carefully in court. It is wise not to use extravagant language, nor to make threats which you do not have the right or intention to carry out. Many months, even years, later you may look somewhat foolish if you are called upon to explain the words you used in the heat of the moment when you wrote the letter before action. It is best to keep to the point, state clearly and concisely the facts of the matter and what you claim, and to be polite.

Because a letter before action may one day be read in court, you should hesitate to include in it any offer to compromise your claim for something less than the full amount. If you did this, it might be an embarrassment to you in court, where you would, in the event, be pressing your claim in full. To get round this difficulty, you can write two letters at the same time, one an ordinary letter before action, and the other a letter written 'without prejudice'. These words at the top of a letter prevent it being produced as evidence in court. A letter written 'without prejudice' can be used to put forward an offer which, if the offer is refused and the case ends up in court after all, would not be disclosed to the judge.

If you go into a shop and complain about faulty goods, nine times out of ten you will get a replacement. On the tenth occasion you meet difficulty. You may be told to get in touch with the manufacturer, or to try some remedy they suggest. Or you may simply be told that they do not take things back. Many people would take a brush-off like this as final, and would assume that nothing further could be done. For those who wish to take the matter further, a letter before action is the next step. Often it produces a satisfactory response, such as an offer of money, or at least an offer to discuss the position. The aim of a letter before action should be to lead to the claim being disposed of amicably.

Writing a letter before action shows that you really mean business, and puts the facts on record. It is not necessary in writing the first letter before action to threaten or even to mention legal proceedings. It is usually best to delay threatening a court action until you have either received no reply to your letter before action or a blank refusal.

The first letter to the other side should read as if you assume that the claim will be met in full, and as if the idea that they would welsh on their liability has not entered your head. On the other hand, it is wise to lay down time limits for a response, so that you are not left wondering whether you have left enough time before proceeding to the next stage.

Emma wrote to Toltons Domestic Appliances Ltd, the manufacturer of the washing machine. Again, she kept a copy.

> *14 Twintree Avenue,*
> *Minford, Surrey*
> *11 December 1972*
>
> *Dear Sirs,*
>
> *It is now seven days since I telephoned your service department about my Washfaster washing machine, asking that your mechanic should come and repair it. He has not come, although I was told that he would be here within a day or two. There have been three previous occasions when the machine has broken down, on two of which there was delay in getting the machine attended to. These breakdowns show that the machine is not up to standard, and I have therefore written to Watsons of High Street, Minford, the shop where I bought the machine, and cancelled my purchase. I have asked them to collect it and to refund the price.*
>
> *In these circumstances, there is no need now for your mechanic to call here. Indeed, if he now calls, I cannot*

allow him to repair the washing machine, as it no longer belongs to me.

I shall be grateful if you will, for the time being, preserve your records relating to this particular machine, especially the record showing the servicing which has been provided since it was bought.

Yours faithfully,

Emma Seaton

Toltons Domestic Appliances Ltd,
349 Godalming Road,
Guildford.

—*response*

Both the letters which Emma had written were ones which could not easily be ignored. The shop was the first to respond. Within three days, Watsons, the department store, replied thus:

Watsons Stores (Minford) Ltd,
High Street,
Minford, Surrey
14th December 1972

Dear Madam,

We are in receipt of your letter, and much regret to learn of the difficulties you have experienced with the Washfaster washing machine purchased from us. We are getting in touch with our suppliers to see what they can do to assist you in putting the matter right, but would advise you that in as much as the difficulties you mention arose through no fault of our company, we regret that we are unable to take back this article as suggested by you. Neither are we able to make a refund to you of the price. We are confident, however, that this machine can be serviced satisfactorily, under the terms of the guarantee and without charge to you at the present time. No doubt you will con-

tact the manufacturers in this regard and we trust that the
article in question can be dealt with to your satisfaction.

Yours faithfully,
K. J. Hurst
Sales Manager

Mrs. E. Seaton.

This polite rebuff displayed an attitude frequently taken by retailers, namely that defects in goods are not their affair, and that the customer should take up the matter with the manufacturers. The truth about the legal responsibility of the seller under the Sale of Goods Act is often unknown to the management and to the sales staff of shops. Many retailers are willing to take goods back if they are returned soon after being purchased, but this is usually done as if it were an act of grace in the interests of good relations with customers. Legally, there is a duty to take something back if it turns out to be substantially defective, and the buyer acts promptly, but none if the customer merely wishes to change it. Shops often do not recognise this distinction, in either case giving the customer the impression that he is being given a favour. Some shops, rather reluctantly, agree to send an article back to the manufacturers. This often implies that only if the manufacturers replace the article can anything be done. It is another way of passing the buck.

Now it was time for Emma to take a firmer line. This was her reply to Watsons:

> *14 Twintree Avenue,*
> *Minford, Surrey.*
> *17 December 1972*

Dear Sir,

Thank you for your letter of 14 December. Legally, you are responsible for this washing machine, not the manufacturers. Under the Sale of Goods Act 1893, I am entitled to cancel a purchase on discovering that the article I bought is substantially defective, and this is what I have done. The trouble in the seven months I owned the machine shows that at the time you sold it to me it was not fit for its intended purpose, nor was it of merchantable quality. This is the basis of my right to cancel my purchase, a right I exercised in my last letter to you, and which still stands. You may, of course, have some redress against your suppliers in view of what has happened, and they in turn may have some redress back along the line, so that ultimately the manufacturers will be involved. But so far as I am concerned, I look to you.

Please remove the washing machine immediately and refund the price I paid, namely £84.50. I need the space it occupies for another machine I intend to buy elsewhere. If I do not hear from you with this sum within 14 days of today's date, I shall have no alternative but to start legal proceedings against you, without further notice or delay. For this purpose, please let me know the address of your registered office and the name and address of the solicitors who, on your behalf, will accept service of those proceedings.

> *Yours faithfully,*
> *Emma Seaton*

Mr. K. J. Hurst,
Sales Manager,
Watsons Stores Ltd.

The useless washing machine was a nuisance, taking up valuable space in the kitchen. Emma Seaton was not entitled to put it out on the pavement, however, even though it no longer belonged to her. It was still in her care and she had to look after it. But having lawfully cancelled her purchase, she was entitled to require the shop to remove their property which was cluttering up her kitchen, once they had repaid her money. She could, if she liked, have made her own arrangements to return it, but obviously she did not wish to part with the machine until the price had been refunded to her; otherwise she might be left in the vulnerable position of being without money or machine. She was entitled to the money and to be relieved of the burden of having the machine in her house, and from a practical point of view she meant to see that both rights were exercised simultaneously.

The terms in which Emma threatened to take the matter to court were similar to those often adopted by solicitors in letters before action written on behalf of clients. She said that she would start legal proceedings 'without further notice or delay' to show that the chances were that the next thing they would receive would be a court summons. This threat did not, however, rule out the possibility of further negotiations.

To show that she really meant business and was familiar with the procedure, she asked for the name and address of the shop's solicitors who would accept on their behalf service of those proceedings. A court summons has to be served on—that is, delivered to—the person or firm being sued, or their solicitors if they have instructions to accept service of the summons on behalf of their client. The last sentence of Emma's letter was intended to show that she was not trying it on, and that if the price was not refunded, she really would sue the shop for it. Finally, the letter, like the previous one, put a time limit on the action to be taken. Two weeks seemed a reasonable time to allow for Watsons to respond to her letter. At the end of that time she would be free to start her court action without having to write any more letters.

Emma quite expected to hear in reply from some solicitors acting for Watsons in the matter. But in fact she heard from the shop itself again. It took the matter no further forward:

> *Watsons Stores (Minford) Ltd,*
> *High Street,*
> *Minford, Surrey.*
> *21st December 1972*

Dear Madam,
> *Washfaster Washing Machine*
> *We duly received your further letter in this matter, but we regret we are unable to assist you. We do not think there is anything we can usefully add to what has already been said, and again suggest that you contact the manufacturers of the machine in question.*
> *Yours faithfully,*
> *S. McNicholas,*
> *Managing Director.*

Mrs. E. Seaton.

In reply to her letter to Toltons, the manufacturer, Emma received nothing more than a printed acknowledgment. No mechanic appeared to do any repairs or servicing. If he had come, Emma would have sent him away.

Further correspondence seemed likely to be futile. The time had come to take action, legal action. That is what Emma and Matthew decided they would do, after considering the risks regarding costs.

costs

The possibility of having to pay the other side's costs if you lose your case is the strongest reason for hesitating to fight a county court case. The legal costs awarded in a county court case are intended to be a partial reimbursement of the amount that the winner has to pay to his lawyers by way of fees, plus out-of-pocket expenses.

The costs the loser has to pay to the winner can amount to a tidy sum. The amount varies enormously, depending on the circumstances. Factors which play a part in increasing or decreasing the amount the loser ends up having to pay include: the total amount at stake; the type of case; the number of witnesses who give evidence; the number and the complications of the documents that are used; whether counsel, that is a barrister, is employed on the winning side; how long the case takes to try; how far away from the court the various parties and their witnesses live or have their offices. Because there are so many differing circumstances in court cases, it is almost impossible to make a general prediction about cases in general, and very hard to predict what the total costs are likely to be in any particular case. Costs can, however, mount up very quickly. A simple case involving, say, one or two witnesses on the winning side, with an amount of

£80 at stake, and a solicitor but no counsel employed, might mean the loser having to pay to the winner costs of between £60 and £70. A larger case, involving, say £200 or so, with many documents, and counsel, with a trial lasting over two days, could easily run up costs of over £150, probably considerably more. On top of this, of course, there is always the losing party's own costs—the amount he has to pay his own lawyers, if any, their out-of-pocket expenses, and his own. Suing for £200, therefore, you may be putting at risk at least that amount again by way of legal costs.

—fixed costs

Sometimes the loser has to pay what are called fixed costs. Most typically, this applies when a defendant pays up more or less as soon as the summons is served on him. Imagine, for example, that I were to get my solicitor to sue an estate agent to recover the sum of £55 wrongfully overcharged, and the estate agent were to pay up as soon as he received the summons. I could recover from the agent—in addition to the £55 and the court fee—a sum of £3 as a contribution towards my solicitor's fees. This £3 is the amount of fixed costs allowed for a claim of £55. Of course, it is almost certain that my solicitor will charge me a good deal more than £3 for the work he has done. But all I can recover from the other side to cover my solicitor's fees for that work is £3, according to the scale of fixed costs. Where the amount claimed is over £100, the amount allowed for fixed costs goes up to £6.

—over £100 at stake

Where the amount at stake in the case is over £100 and the case is not settled at once, the costs may be either assessed or taxed. When costs are assessed, it means that the judge makes a quick, somewhat rough and ready, estimate of the total costs that ought to be allowed, on the basis of what he thinks was necessary for the winning of the case. The amount allowed for each step in preparing and fighting the case in court increases according to the amount at stake in the case. He usually uses a scale as a basis for working out the costs.

If the case has been not at all straightforward, the likelihood is that the costs will be taxed. Where this happens, the judge makes an order at the end of the trial, awarding costs on one of the scales, leaving the actual amount of costs to be worked out later precisely, item by item, at a hearing called a taxation.

If your claim is for something not much over £100, it may be worth reducing it to £100, so that the amount of your opponent's costs which you have to pay if you lose is much reduced. (Another reason for reducing a claim in this way is that for cases up to £100 arbitration can apply even if the other side objects.)

—over £5 and up to £100 at stake

Where the amount at stake is over £5 and up to £100, not more than £3 is allowed by way of solicitor's charges. This is meant to cover the cost of having a solicitor issue the summons (although no solicitor would do it for so little). No costs of having a solicitor (or counsel for that matter) to take the case in court are generally allowed in cases involving £100 or under. It follows from this that if you sue for a sum of not more than £100, the amount you risk having to pay, if you lose, is not very much. It amounts, at worst, to a sum of up to £5 for the court fee on issuing the summons, plus the other side's witnesses expenses and allowances. If you are being sued and lose the case, there could, in addition, be up to £3 solicitor's charges for the other side.

—up to £5 at stake
Where the amount claimed is £5 or less, no solicitor's fees can be recovered from the loser, even if a solicitor is employed to take your case. For instance, if you sue a shop, say, over a pair of shoes costing £4·95, and the shop defends the case, employing a solicitor to fight you every inch of the way, the whole of the solicitor's fees incurred by the shop will have to be paid by the shop, even if you lose your case completely. The only amount you could have to pay would be the court fee you paid to start the case (£1), plus witnesses' allowances and travelling expenses for the other side.

The county court is not just a court room where a judge sits and tries cases all day long. It is the centre of a local system of justice, with a court office, staff, and a procedure for coping with a variety of cases. The court has, if need be, the power to enforce its decisions, as by seizing and selling a debtor's possessions, and even sometimes by sending a person to prison if he fails to obey a court order.

The county court deals only with civil cases, that is claims by one citizen against another, a citizen for this purpose including a company or firm. There are broadly speaking two main functions of the county court. Firstly, it forces people to pay their debts. Secondly, it provides a means of settling disputes. County courts also deal with adoption orders and some similar family matters and, in some courts outside London, with divorce cases.

In many towns there is a separate county court building. To find the address, look up under 'Courts' in the phone book, and find the subheading 'County Courts'. The building where the county court is situated may house other courts as well, so outside it may just say 'The Law Courts' or something like that. You may find that the magistrates court (which deals mainly with criminal cases) is there also. If so, the administration of the different sorts of court is kept quite separate, but they may share some of the facilities, including the use of the court rooms.

county courts
A county court consists of two things: firstly, a number of rooms which comprise the court complex,

made up of one or more court rooms, some offices, waiting rooms, rooms for solicitors and barristers, consultation rooms and so on; and secondly, a number of people. Every county court has a judge and a registrar (an assistant judge), both of whom are qualified lawyers. Their function is to try the disputed cases and give judgment. The court staff are civil servants. In charge of the administration is a chief clerk with a number of clerks, typists, bailiffs and ushers under him. The court rooms may be attached to the court office, or situated in a public building such as the town hall. The county court is there to provide a vital public service, namely the administration of justice, and nobody should feel hesitant about using the county court, when the need arises. Court officials ought to be pleased to find people wanting to make use of the facilities they have to offer. The courts are there to be used.

In theory, it would be very nice if, as soon as a dispute arose between two people, they could go straight off to a judge and get the matter decided, without any delay or formality. In many states in the USA, there are special small claims courts, where disputes involving small amounts can be disposed of in this way, without any formality, quickly and cheaply. There is no prospect of that happening here, in this country, so the county court has been adapted to cope with small claims.

An unofficial arbitration scheme for small claims is in operation in Manchester and London (Westminster). These have been of great value, and show that it can be possible to deal with small claims by a simple procedure cheaply and satisfactorily. But such schemes are neither widespread nor official. The main drawback with them is that they do not have the power to compel traders, or indeed anyone else, to submit. They lack the force of law.

We therefore have to make do with what we have got. The county courts were set up in 1846, as people's courts, where justice could be swiftly and cheaply obtained without great formality or expense. But, in time, formality became piled upon formality so that the unaided layman was at a disadvantage in the county court, and for years the only laymen who have appeared there regularly have been unfortunates who got into debt. In recent times, however, the formalities have been eased, and procedure simplified.

—procedure

Before a claim reaches the stage of being heard, some procedures must be gone through. The plaintiff (the person bringing the case) has to put into writing the exact nature of his claim, in a document called particulars of claim. Likewise, if the defendant (the person against whom the case is brought), wishes to dispute what is alleged in the particulars of claim, he must set out the details in his written defence. The purpose of this is to identify the precise matters which are disputed, with a view to saving time.

For example, imagine the plaintiff shopkeeper alleges in his particulars of claim that he sold some goods to the defendant consumer at a stated price. The defendant does not deny the sale, but claims that the goods were faulty. In this case the defence, put in by the defendant, admits the sale, but says that the goods were not up to standard. In this way, the plaintiff (shopkeeper) knows that he does not have to prove the facts about the sale—they have been admitted by the defendant. Only facts which are not admitted have to be proved. The particulars of claim and the defence are called pleadings.

Another object in having pleadings is to prevent one side taking the other side by surprise at the trial. It would waste time and increase costs for all concerned if one side could suddenly spring some new allegation, without giving advance notice of it to his opponent. It might be advantageous tactically, but would not serve the ends of justice. He therefore must declare his hand in advance, so that his opponent has a reasonable opportunity of knowing what case he has to meet, and of bringing evidence to refute allegations that are not admitted.

There are other procedures which sometimes apply and which are designed to prevent either side being taken by surprise. By what is called discovery of documents, for instance, each side, in advance of the court hearing, is allowed to study the documents which the other side will be producing at the trial. In this way it is not possible to have a document suddenly flung at you by your opponent which torpedoes the case you are making, at the hearing in court.

Another means of trying to sort out the issues in a case in advance of the actual court hearing is called the pre-trial review. The registrar of the court holds an informal pre-trial hearing, at which both sides should be present or represented. If either side fails to appear, the case may go by default against him. If the plaintiff fails to appear, his claim may be struck out——that means he cannot proceed with his claim; if the defendant does not appear, judgment may be given against him there and then without a trial.

If both sides attend the pre-trial review, the registrar goes into the questions that arise for decision in the case, and sees what needs to be done in order to dispose of the case in a way which is 'just, expeditious and economical'. He will decide whether discovery of documents is necessary or not. The registrar may well be able to get each side to agree about some of the matters which, out of caution, were disputed according to the pleadings. He may well be able to make helpful suggestions about how the case ought to proceed and to tidy up any loose ends arising from the way the parties have dealt with the case so far. The pre-trial review can result in the case being settled there and then. Or, if the case does not involve more than £100, the registrar is likely to refer the dispute to arbitration.

All this procedure may sound formidable. But in the county court, there is often very little formality. Pleadings need not be expressed in legal language. Very often there is no need for discovery of documents at all, and time limits are not strictly enforced. If there are any gaps or errors in the procedure, the chances are that they can be put right at the pre-trial review. Nobody should be put off from suing in the county court by fear of complex procedure, even if the case is not referred to the county court arbitration service.

a visit to the county court

Emma and Matthew discussed the prospect that faced them on bringing a claim against Watsons in the local county court. They looked up the address of the court in the phone book. Emma phoned the court office to find out when the court was sitting, what hours the office was open, and for confirmation that she did not have to have a solicitor. The clerk on the phone reassured her.

A few days later, she went to the court building to watch the court in action. Her friend Judy went with her to give her moral support. Hearings began at 10.30 in the morning. There were two courts sitting, one in the judge's court, the other in the registrar's court. Emma visited the judge's court and sat listening to what was happening for nearly half an hour. The judge was robed in a purple gown, and wore a wig. From the back of the court where she sat, Emma had a view of the heads of the lawyers whose cases were being dealt with. The case that was under way as she sat listening was a dispute in which a landlord was claiming possession of a flat from the tenant. The landlord was represented by a barrister (who was referred to in court as counsel), and the barrister wore a wig and a black gown. The tenant was represented by a solicitor, who also wore a gown, but no wig. Emma tried to pick up the threads of what was going on, and gathered that the case hinged on the alleged misbehaviour of the tenant, who was being asked questions about the goings on in the flat, firstly by his own solicitor, and then (under cross-examination) by counsel for the landlord. From time to time the judge intervened for clarification of a point. Sitting listening for half an hour, Emma got the flavour of court procedure, and an idea of what would be involved if her own case came to trial.

It is a fundamental rule of justice in this country that court cases should be tried in public, so that anyone can wander in and sit and listen to what is going on. In addition, of course, the press are entitled to be there, to make a note of what is said, and to report the proceedings in the newspapers. In practice, there is often no member of the public listening to a case in a county court. If there is anybody, the chances are that he or she is concerned in a case that will be heard later that day, and is just passing the time listening to the present case. There is nothing to stop anybody listening merely out of curiosity. Nobody will stop you if you turn up for a county court trial and it is very important that nobody should.

Some hearings connected with court cases are held in private, however. When this happens, the hearing is said to be 'in chambers'. This often happens with the pre-trial review. Some county court cases, such as those involving the adoption of children, and disputes about the custody of children in divorce cases, are also held in chambers. Often, proceedings in chambers are conducted in the private room of the judge or registrar. In other cases, proceedings in chambers are held in the normal court room, especially if both sides are represented by solicitors and counsel, so that there would not be enough room to accommodate everybody in a private room. When this happens, the court is said to be sitting in chambers, and it may well be that there is a notice pinned up outside saying 'in chambers'. This means you cannot go in, and that if by mistake you were to go in, you would be told to leave. These are the exceptions, however, and the trial of the great majority of cases that are heard in the county court is held in public and this means that anybody is entitled, by law, to be present.

After leaving the judge's court, Emma visited the court office and spoke to one of the clerks there. She explained that she had a claim against a local shop and intended to bring a case in the county court if necessary. The clerk was helpful and explained what she would have to do in order to get the case going: decide which summons to issue, complete a form called a request, find out the registered address of the company she was suing, and prepare the particulars of claim.

County courts have available a government booklet called *Small claims in the county court*. This explains the procedure and includes a specimen of some of the documents, including the particulars of claim. The booklet is available free of charge to anyone who asks for it, and can also be obtained from Citizens Advice Bureaux and from consumer advice centres.

which summons
Every county court case begins with either a default summons or an ordinary summons. If a precise sum is claimed, a default summons is used. This applies, for example, when a shop is suing for an unpaid debt or a person is seeking to recover the sum of money

he lent to a friend. In such cases, the plaintiff's claim is said to be liquidated, that means fixed or ascertained in amount. But if, for example, a person were claiming compensation for being injured in a road accident, he would not be claiming a fixed amount from the start, but would be claiming for however much he could get, it being a matter for the judge to decide at the hearing exactly how much. Such a claim is said to be unliquidated, and the plaintiff is said to be claiming unliquidated damages. Such a case is begun by ordinary summons.

Emma considered what sort of summons to issue. When she got down to it, and worked out the figures, it transpired that most of the items she would be claiming could be precisely calculated. These included the price she paid for the washing machine. But she was also entitled to compensation for the inconvenience of being without the use of her washing machine while it had broken down. How much money she ought to receive for something as vague as inconvenience is a matter of opinion, so that for this item she would just claim damages, not a specific figure. This was an unliquidated claim, and put her case, therefore, into the category demanding an ordinary summons, even though the most important item for which she was claiming was in fact liquidated, namely the refund of the purchase price of the washing machine.

which county court

Emma next pondered the question of where Watsons Stores (Minford) Ltd, the proposed defendant, had its registered office. You cannot just bring a case in the most convenient county court from your point of view. You have to show some connection between the case and the district covered by the particular county court. If you bought the goods in the district of the court you have in mind, so that technically the contract was made within that district, that is sufficient to give that county court power to deal with the case. Alternatively, if the defendant lives, or (in the case of a limited company) has its registered office in the county court district, that is enough to give the court jurisdiction. But even if you are relying on the place where the purchase was made to give the court you choose the power to deal with your case, it is still necessary to state in the court forms exactly where the defendant resides, carries on business or, in the case of a limited company, has its registered office.

If you are suing an individual whose home address is in the district for the county court you choose, you have in any event chosen the right county court. If you are suing a man who owns a shop, you can sue him in the county court district where the shop is or in the county court district where he lives; it would be similar if the shop were run by two or more partners (but not a limited company)—you could sue in a court of a district where any one of the partners lives. But if the shop or business is a limited company (that is, the word limited is the last word of the name under which the business is run), you may sue them in the county court for the place where the contract was made or the county court for the district where they have their registered office. The registered office might be the head office of the company but it is not necessarily so. In the case of a large company, the chances are that the address will be miles away from the place where the local shop is. It will probably be in London, but could be anywhere else in England or Wales. It could be in the office of some chartered accountant or solicitor who acted for the company when it was first formed.

Since January 1973 every limited company must state on its letterheads and order forms the address of its registered office. So, in the first place, look there.

But if a company does not yet comply with this law, there are other ways of finding out the address of the registered office of the company. You could ask them. They do not have to reply, but if they do, you are entitled to take what they say at face value. If this does not work, you can find out the registered office of a limited company by enquiring on the phone from the Department of Trade at Companies House in the City of London. You phone 01-253 9253 and give the name of the company. You will be told the registered number of the company and when your call is transferred, you quote this number and are given the address of the registered office of the company.

There can easily be confusion about the name of a company, and it is important to get the name right when suing it, as there are many thousands of companies, some of which have similar names. But no two companies have exactly the same name and every company is required by law to state its correct name on its writing paper, and on invoices, bills and suchlike. Sometimes a company carries on business under a name which is different from its official name. Brownings' of Amersham turn out, on closer scrutiny, to be Browning (Ironmongers) Limited; John Lewis is really John Lewis and Company Limited. It is important to be right.

You may be uncertain whether the business you are concerned with is a limited company or not. What if the firm you have been dealing with just says on its literature and letter headings: "Minford Tyres and Batteries" and nothing more, except the address? In practice this happens quite often, although it is illegal. Every firm has by law to state on its letter headings, invoices and other business literature the correct name of its proprietor. This means that if it is a limited company, the correct name of the company must appear. If it is a business trading under an invented name (such as Acme Electrics, or Riverside Boarding Kennels), the names of the individuals who are the proprietors must be stated on headed stationery. If it is not, they are acting unlawfully. But there is a register you can search (in person for a fee of 5p; not by post), that may give the information. This is called the register of business names, and is also kept at Companies House, 71 City Road, London EC1. Any business which is carried on under a name which is not the name of the actual proprietor has to be registered there. But due to weak enforcement of the law about this, many are not registered which ought to be. If you do not get the name right, the firm may turn round and say 'That's not us, so we are not going to take any notice of this summons'. It is, however, possible to amend the court papers so that the correct name appears, when later on you discover it. The best thing to do is to make a conscious effort to get the right name, and to check the particulars from letters, bills or receipts, and what appears on the front of the premises where the business is carried on.

Getting the correct address of your opponent is important not only for the purpose of finding out which county court is the right one to bring the case in. It is also important from the point of view of service of the summons. That is, the court will want to know where to send the summons, so that the defendant gets it in a way which cannot be ignored. Nine times out of ten you will be safe putting as the firm's address the address of the shop or showroom where you actually did business with them.

When you are suing a firm or businees which is not a limited company, you may, if you like, put on the court papers the name of the firm, without including the name or names of the individuals who own it. An example of the correct way to describe such a firm on official court papers would therefore be 'Acme Electrics (a firm)'. If you do know the name of the proprietors, it is correct to say 'Bruce G. Macgeorge trading as Acme Electrics' or 'Mr. J. K. Anderson and Mrs. B. K. Thomas trading as Robert Simpson & Co.'. The individuals who own a firm are responsible for the firm's liabilities irrespective of whether it is sued in its name or in the names of the individuals.

In the case of a limited company, however, the individuals running the company are not responsible for the company's debts; only the company itself is liable. The liability of the shareholders, including the directors, is indeed limited in that way, hence the word. In the case of a limited company, therefore, you use the name of the company, with the word limited at the end. In the case of the gas corporation, electricity boards or other nationalised outfits, you can sue them in their full name, as it appears on the bill you receive.

If you are suing a person, and you know his full name, use that. If you know part of his name, put down all that you know, adding 'Mr.' or 'Ms'.

To find out if a particular address is covered by a particular county court, ring up the office of the county court and enquire.

particulars of claim

Having decided the particular county court you will use for your case, you should next prepare the details of your claim in the way the court requires it. This is done in a document called particulars of claim, which sets out, paragraph by paragraph, the main facts of your case, followed by a statement summarising the essential legal basis of your claim, and ending up with the amount of your claim. You should prepare your particulars of claim on your own piece of paper. There is no printed form for it. The court will need two copies, and you will need another one to keep, so you will want an original plus two copies. If you are suing two firms (the travel as well as the tour operator, for instance), you will have to provide an extra copy of the particulars of claim. It is obviously better if it is typed rather than handwritten, but there is no rule to exclude handwritten particulars of claim.

Equally, there is no rule to say that you must adopt the formal legal language that is used when the document is prepared by a lawyer.

This is what Emma did. For her case against Watsons, she drafted the particulars of claim in rough at first, then improved the wording by editing the draft with care. Then, when she could think of no more alterations that could be made to it, she typed it out (with two carbons). This is how it read:

IN THE MINFORD COUNTY COURT

Plaint No..........

Between

Mrs. Emma Caroline Seaton   *Plaintiff*
    and
Watsons Stores (Minford) Limited   *Defendant*

Particulars of claim

1. At the beginning of May 1972, I ordered a De Luxe model Washfaster clothes-washing machine from the defendant, Watsons Stores (Minford) Limited, at their department store at 12 High Street, Minford, Surrey. The price was £84·50.

2. Watsons delivered the washing machine to my house at 14 Twintree Avenue, Minford, in about the middle of May 1972 and installed it there.

3. Within about 7 days from when the new machine was installed, it broke down. Due to some defect in the mechanism the water was not pumped out at the appropriate point in the cycle of operations started by turning the control knob. As a result, it was not possible to pump out the water, so it remained in the machine and my clothes were left completely wet. To get these clothes dry, I

had to take them out by hand and extract as much water as I could by hand, and then put them out to dry. This was inconvenient and unpleasant.

4. I immediately telephoned the nearest service centre of the manufacturer, Toltons Domestic Appliances Ltd, at Guildford. By the terms of their 'Guarantee' delivered to me when the machine was new, Toltons had accepted certain responsibilities regarding faults in the machine. I told Toltons on the telephone of the breakdown of the machine and asked for someone to come and mend it. The person at the other end of the phone said that someone would come but could not say when this would be.

5. I telephoned Toltons several times in the next two weeks, but did not receive any satisfactory information about when their mechanic would call. In the meantime, in order to do the washing for my family (my husband, myself and my two children, aged 9 and 6), I had to go to the local launderette about three times, costing on average 50p each time. Eventually the mechanic from Toltons called without warning about two weeks after I had reported the breakdown to them, fixed the machine and for a time after that it worked normally.

6. About two months later, in August 1972, the machine broke down again. This time there was a loud rumbling noise in the machine when the washing action began, which sounded so alarming that I turned it off and did not use it again until a mechanic from Toltons called after a few days, and replaced various parts. I was again involved in inconvenience, unpleasantness and expense at the launderette.

7. The machine worked normally again for a time, but after the second visit from the mechanic it did not seem to deal with the washing as well as it had done previously. Then in the middle of October 1972 the machine broke down a third time, the trouble being inability to pump out

water once again. I phoned Toltons, and it was over two weeks before their mechanic came, despite several phone calls. The mechanic was unable to repair the machine there and then, as he did not have the necessary spare part. He called again about three days later, fixed the machine, and then it worked normally, more or less, for a while.

8. On 4 December 1972 the machine broke down again. This time the machinery and control system continued to operate, but some connection carrying the water away became dislodged, with the result that soiled water poured all over the floor of the kitchen. As soon as I discovered this had happened, I switched off the machine and tried to clear up the mess. The floor was damaged and I was put to a great deal of trouble, misery and inconvenience.

9. Since then I have not attempted to use the machine. I have been going to the launderette to get my washing done and incurring expense as a result.

10. I phoned Toltons on 4 December to come to repair the machine. The person at the other end of the phone could not say when the mechanic would call.

11. After waiting 7 days with no visit from the mechanic, I wrote to Watsons informing them of the trouble I have had, and, relying on my legal rights, cancelled my purchase from them of the machine, asked them to pay back the money I paid for it, to remove it from my house and to compensate me for the expense I had incurred.

12. Watsons replied by letter dated 14 December 1972. They refused to refund the price, to take back the machine or to pay me compensation. Since then they have again refused to do so.

13. The machine I bought from Watsons was defective when delivered to me, as is shown by the breakdowns that happened, as detailed above. Because of this I say that the machine did not comply with the requirements of the Sale of Goods Act 1893, and that Watsons were in breach of

the implied terms of the contract of sale in supplying a defective machine, so entitling me to cancel the contract, to claim back the price and to be compensated.

14. I therefore claim:

(1) a refund of £84.50, which was the price I paid for the machine. Alternatively, I claim damages of up to £84.50;

(2) damages for breach of contract consisting of:

(i) expenses incurred so far through breakdowns in the machine, namely:

—12 visits to the launderette at average of 50p each visit	£6.00
—bus fares, petrol and other travelling expenses	£1.00
—10 phone calls	0.40
—damage to kitchen floor	£5.00
	£12.40

(ii) compensation for loss of use, inconvenience, upset, unpleasantness and trouble; future expenses at the launderette and for travelling, and other loss and inconvenience resulting to me from the breakdowns in the machine (up to £50)

(3) Costs

Dated 1973

to:

The registrar of the court and to the defendant

(signed) Emma C. Seaton

Emma Caroline Seaton,
of 14 Twintree Avenue,
Minford, Surrey,
the plaintiff, who will
accept service of all
proceedings at that address.

A shortened version of these particulars of claim, which would not spell out the full drama in such detail, would also be acceptable. It would look like this:

IN THE MINFORD COUNTY COURT

Plaint No..........

Between

Mrs. Emma Caroline Seaton   *Plaintiff*
    and
Watsons Stores (Minford) Limited   *Defendant*

Particulars of claim

1. I bought a Washfaster washing machine from Watsons Stores (the defendant) in May 1972, costing £84.50. They installed it.

2. On at least three occasions between May and December 1972 it went wrong and stopped working, the first time within a week of when I had it. It was 'put right' each time by Toltons Domestic Appliances Ltd, the manufacturer, under their guarantee, but it was always unreliable.

3. It finally went wrong on 4 December 1972, when it started to pump water all over the floor of my kitchen, damaging the floor.

4. I wrote to Watsons cancelling the purchase on 11 December 1972, asking for my money back, for them to take away the machine and to compensate me. They refused.

5. The washing machine is defective and has been ever since I first had it. This gives me the right to cancel the purchase (which I did) and to get my money back and to receive compensation, under the Sale of Goods Act 1893.

This I now claim, as follows:

(1) refund of price paid (or compensation)   £84.50
(2) out of pocket expenses:
    (a) launderette charges   6.00

(b) bus fares, petrol and other minor
expenses   1.00
(c) 10 phone calls   0.40
(d) damage to kitchen floor   5.00
(3) compensation for loss of use,
inconvenience, continuing expenses for
washing and travelling (up to £50)
(4) costs

Dated 1973

To the registrar   (Signed) Emma C. Seaton
of the court   of 14 Twintree Avenue,
and to the   Minford, Surrey,
defendant   the plaintiff, who
                                       will accept service of
                                       all proceedings at that
                                                       address.

Whether to use a long or a short version of your
particulars of claim depends on the circumstances. If
you expect your claim to be contested seriously, that
is, if you have had a sensible reply from your adversary disputing the facts or the legal situation such as
to suggest to you that the claim will be fought, the
longer version is probably better. It sets out the
history step by step. But if you have the impression
that, when he receives your county court summons,
your adversary will give way quickly, without disputing the case, there is less need for detail and you
might use a short version.

The particulars of claim starts, as does every official court document connected with the case, with the
title of action. The top left hand corner always says:

'In the.................County Court', to identify the particular county court in which the case is proceeding. Alongside that on the right hand side it says: 'Plaint No.............'. Every case has its own plaint number, which will be filled in there by the clerk at the county court office when the action is begun. This number is the court's official reference number for the case, and should be quoted in all letters and documents about the case. The court keeps no alphabetical index of its cases and so cannot trace its records without knowing the number of the case.

Then follows the rest of the title of the case: 'Between Mrs. Emma Caroline Seaton, Plaintiff' it says. She is the person bringing the case, so she is the plaintiff, the person with the complaint. It then says: '. . . . and Watsons Stores (Minford) Ltd, Defendant'. They are the ones against whom the case is being brought, so they are the defendant, the one who is being brought to the court to defend the claim.

The particulars of claim is a document intended to set before the court and to give the defendant the precise nature of the plaintiff's claim. The relevant facts, beginning at the beginning, are set out in numbered paragraphs. Even obvious things should be stated, so that the story is complete in itself. You should spell it out preferably in chronological order, and each new step in the story deserves a new numbered paragraph. The point of this is to identify more readily the various bits of what is involved in the case, so that the defendant can, when preparing his defence, easily state what facts he admits and what facts he disputes. He may say, for instance: 'Paragraphs 1 and 2 of the particulars of claim are admitted. Paragraphs 3 to 13 inclusive are denied . . . .'

Only relevant facts ought to be stated. There is no point in including things like: 'This made me very angry . . . .' or 'My neighbour told me I ought not to put up with it any longer . . . .'. You do not have to apologise for or justify yourself in troubling the court with a claim. If you have a legal right that has not been honoured, you can bring the matter to court, without having to explain your motives.

Among the facts to state are details of expenses and losses suffered as a result of the trouble that has given rise to the case. The actual amounts spent are listed at the end, as in Emma Seaton's case, but in the body of the document it is a good idea to include, as you go along, the fact that 'this put me to the expense of having to . . . .' or 'as a result I suffered loss or damage in that . . . .', and then describe what you had to do, involving loss or expense.

Having set out the facts, you then draw them all together by formally stating what you say is the legal result of them. In Emma Seaton's case, in the long version, she said in paragraph 13 that the machine was defective and so did not comply with the Sale of Goods Act. This is the hub of her case, and sums up the way she puts her claim before the court.

Finally, she sets out what she is claiming, in money terms. It is generally a case of asking for money, for there is not much else that courts can give to people who have had a raw deal. There are, however, cases where courts make useful orders apart from ordering money to be paid. A landlord, for instance, may seek an order for possession from his tenant, which could end up with the court bailiff physically evicting the tenant. And if a person persistently infringes someone else's rights, as when one person starts encroaching on his neighbour's land with a new building, the court can stop this by issuing an injunction (that is, a court order to stop doing something) with the threat of imprisonment in case of refusal to obey. If you seek an injunction, you ask for it at the end of your particulars of claim. You might use these words: 'Therefore I claim damages of £X and an injunction to restrain the defendant from continuing to trespass on my land', or: '. . . . and an injunction to restrain the defendant from playing the trombone after midnight.' Injunctions are nearly always granted to stop someone from doing something rather than to compel someone to do something. You can ask for an injunction only if you are also claiming damages.

In consumer cases, it is not likely that the question of an injunction will arise. It will almost always be a question of claiming money and nothing more. Even if, for example, a shop refuses to repair or supply a spare part for a defective appliance, you still do not ask for an injunction requiring him to do these things. For one thing, under the law of contract his only obligation is to compensate you, not to put the thing right. Secondly, courts are reluctant to grant injunctions anyway, and will only do so when compensation in money terms is not an adequate remedy.

damages

Claims for money in court cases are either claims for

debt or claims for damages. Where you are suing for repayment of a sum you lent to somebody, or for the price of something you sold, you are suing for a debt—a definite sum which someone promised to pay you. Damages consist of compensation, that is, paying you back for expenses or losses you have incurred, or compensating you for loss, injury or damage you have sustained. Damages in this sense are either special or general. Special damages consist of precise amounts already calculated, items which you have incurred as expenditure or loss which you can pinpoint in amount.

In Emma's case, the items of special damage were the charges at the launderette (£6), the bus fares, petrol and other travelling expenses estimated at £1 and the 10 phone calls costing 40p. A sum is special damage even if it is only an estimate, in the sense that the actual amount may be a precise sum, but is not exactly known, so an estimate is put in.

But in the case of general damages there is no precise known amount that is being claimed. Instead there is a general loss or damage suffered, which will be compensated by a round sum, to be awarded by the judge.

In Emma's case, the compensation for inconvenience, loss of use, upset and the trouble resulting from the breakdowns in the washing machine was an item of general damage. It included an ingredient consisting of future expenses incurred through having to use the launderette to do her washing. This illustrates the difference between special and general damages quite neatly. The launderette expenses incurred so far could be calculated exactly—12 visits at 50p a visit is £6. But there could be further ones. It depended on when the case ended and Watsons paid up. The future launderette expenses, being incapable of precise calculation, therefore became part of her claim for general damages.

It is often not possible to put in a figure for the amount you calculate you should get. You have to say: 'I claim damages for this', and leave the court to award an appropriate amount. But it is advisable to put in a figure as the maximum you claim for general damages. This is for two reasons. Firstly, because you have to pay a court fee when you start a county court case and you pay according to the amount you are claiming. If you do not put in a sum as the top limit of the amount claimed, you have to pay a higher fee, to cover the maximum amount you could theoretically get. This would be more than if you made a realistic estimate of the probable maximum sum you could get for general damages. Secondly, it is advisable to limit your claim in case you lose. The costs the loser has to pay depend on the amount of the claim: the higher the claim, the higher the costs. Thus Emma says in the final part of her particulars of claim: 'I claim . . . . compensation for loss of use, inconvenience . . . . (up to £50).'

asking for arbitration
From October 1973, small claims can be dealt with by the county court arbitration scheme. In contrast with a trial in court, arbitration means that the case is dealt with in private, informally, and that strict rules of evidence and procedure need not apply.

Where no more than £100 is at stake, arbitration can be ordered even if one side objects. If over £100 is at stake, both sides must agree.

If you want your case to be dealt with by arbitration, you can ask for this at the end of your particulars of claim, irrespective of the amount involved. If in doubt, ask for arbitration.

issuing the summons

As a result of including a claim for damages in her claim, Emma could not issue a default summons. A default summons has the advantage that, if your opponent does not contest your claim, you may be able to obtain a court order for the payment of your claim—it is called a judgment—without having to attend court at all after issuing the summons: if no defence is sent within 14 days from the date the summons is received by the defendant, the case goes by default against the defendant. This is obviously a good thing from the plaintiff's point of view, as it saves the inconvenience, not to mention the strain on the nervous system, of having to attend a court hearing. However, a default summons can only be used where the exact amount of the claim is ascertained in advance (technically known as liquidated). Emma therefore had to use an ordinary summons. She thought it not worth confining her claim to only getting the price of her machine back, just for the sake of the advantage, such as it is, of being able to use a default summons.

Emma had found out that the registered office of Watsons Stores (Minford) Limited was at 148 Buckingham Street, Guildford, that is, not within the district covered by the Minford County Court. This meant that she would be suing a defendant whose address was outside the district of the court, and accordingly would have to rely on the place of purchase to give the Minford County Court the right to deal with her case. This also affected the question of which form of 'request' she would have to ask for at the court office. In her case it would be the form of request for an ordinary summons (as opposed to a default summons) for a case where the defendant was out of the district (as opposed to one for a defendant in the district).

Now she could proceed to the next stage, the actual issue of the summons. Before leaving home, she made sure she had all the papers about the case.

Inside the main hall of the county court building was a door marked *County Court Office*, and in she went, her mouth a little dry with excitement. Inside was a counter beyond which stretched the usual paraphernalia of any office—desks, phones, filing cabinets, a few tea cups. There was a notice telling anyone who bothered to read it how to get legal aid, and one saying that 'The staff in this office are not in a position to give legal advice. They will however assist in the completion of court forms and explain the procedures involved on request'.

'I've come to issue a county court summons. I don't have a solicitor, and I haven't done it before. I wonder if you can help me,' she said. The clerk eyed her bundle of papers a bit suspiciously. She did not seem to be a nut case or a trouble-maker. 'We aren't allowed to give legal advice, you know,' he said, wondering if he was going to be late for his lunch for the third time that week.

'I know you aren't,' replied Emma, smiling at him. 'I have brought my particulars of claim, one for you and one for the defendant. And I've kept one for myself, of course. But there is this form I need. I believe it is called a request, is that right?'

'Yes, a request, madam,' said the clerk. 'There are several different kinds. Which one do you want?'

'That's where I want your help,' said Emma. 'Now, so far as I can make out, there are two points which matter. First of all, mine is not a claim for a fixed sum of money—look. I am claiming compensation and therefore not a liquidated sum, as you call it.'

The clerk could see now that she did know a little of what she was talking about. 'You should make it an ordinary summons,' he said.

'That's what I thought,' said Emma.

'Where's your defendant? That's the next point,' continued the clerk.

'Well, it's a company,' replied Emma 'and the registered office is outside this court's district. In fact, its at Guildford, I found out.'

'I see,' he said 'then how do you reckon this court's got jurisdiction?'

'Because the facts arose here,' said Emma. 'It is a claim for breach of contract, a contract of purchase made from a shop in the High Street, here in Minford. It was Watsons, as a matter of fact, and it's them that I am suing.' The clerk looked a bit startled.

'Right. Well that will be okay then,' said the clerk. 'This is the form of request you need.' He produced a white form entitled: '8–Praecipe for Ordinary Summons against Defendant out of District'.

request

Emma gazed at the form in awe. It looked offputting, full of small print, and sadly jargon-laden. The first point she observed was that it was called a praecipe and not a request. Before March 1972, the form used to be called a praecipe; the name was officially changed as a gesture in the direction of making county courts easier for laymen to use. But quite a number of the old forms are still around, waiting for stocks to be used up. Even where the new form of request is available, the layout and wording remain much the same. Only the name is changed. On closer examination, however, Emma found that the form was not quite so formidable after all. In essence it was merely asking for the full name and address of both sides in the case, the plaintiff and the defendant, and seeking to establish how it was claimed that this particular court could handle the case.

At the top it said: 'In the .... County Court'; Emma had no difficulty in completing that part by inserting the word Minford.

Then came the panel headed 'Statement of Parties', beginning with 'Plaintiff's names in full, residence or place of business and occupation'. That was not difficult. She completed the panel with her own full name and address: 'Emma Caroline Seaton, 14 Twintree Avenue, Minford, Surrey, housewife.' Then the form said 'If a female, state whether married, single, or a widow.' She put married.

The form described what else a plaintiff must say, where the circumstances are peculiar. 'If suing in a representative capacity, state in what capacity'. This referred to cases such as an executor of somebody's will suing for money lent by the deceased. Then the form said: 'If an infant required to sue by a next friend, state that fact, and names in full, residence or place of business, and occupation of next friend.' One has heard of a best friend, and supposedly a next best friend. But a next friend? It is in fact the legal title for someone who represents a minor—someone under 18—in bringing a court case on the minor's behalf.

Then the form referred to the possibility of the plaintiff being an assignee. 'If an assignee, state that fact, and name, address and occupation of assignor'. This could arise in the following way. A shop sells goods on credit to someone who turns out to be a defaulter. The shop pressures him to pay, but he ignores the letters that are written. After doing everything it can, short of going to court, the shop decides to abandon its efforts to get the money itself. So it sells the debt to a debt collector for, say, 50 per cent of its face value. The debt collector buys the right to sue the defaulter, taking his chances on successfully getting the money. As a result, the debt is assigned to

c

the debt collector, who would then bring a court action in his own name, as assignee, for the amount owing.

Then the form of request dealt with the possibility of partners in a firm suing for a debt. 'If co-partners suing in the name of their firm, add "Suing as a Firm".' This covered cases where a business which is not a limited company but is carried on by two or more partners in business together, sues for a debt.

The last possibility dealt with in the part of the form for the plaintiff's particulars was this: 'If a company registered under the Companies Act, 1948, state the address of the registered office and describe it as such'.

There was a similar variety of possibilities in the part of the form devoted to describing the defendant, the person against whom the case was being brought. Much of it echoed what had been asked in relation to the plaintiff, just above. 'Defendant's surname and (where known) his or her initials or names in full; defendant's residence or place of business (if a proprietor of the business).' In other words: name and address and particulars of person being sued, giving full names where you know them, or initials if you do not. Then it continued: 'Whether male or female, and if female, whether Mrs or Miss'. You do not have to state the sex of your opponent if it is obvious. You do not have to say 'William George Adamson (male)' even though the form implied that you did. But if you do not know the defendant's full names but only, say, the initials, and you do know his or her sex, then you do state his or her sex. You say: 'Mr J. K. Roberts' or Mrs D. J. Chafer', always giving what information you can on this score. It does not matter if you do not know, you just leave it blank.

Then the form said: 'Whether an infant (where known)'. Again, this means a minor, a person under 18. There are complications when suing a person under 18. First of all, he may not necessarily be liable in the way an adult is, as special legal rules apply, especially so far as contracts are concerned. Then it may not be worth suing a young person, even if he is legally liable, simply because he may not have the money to pay. But if you sue a minor, you state on the form the fact that he is a minor. The person who represents a minor against whom a court case is brought is called a guardian ad litem.

Then the form asked for the defendant's 'Occupation (where known)'. That only applies to individuals, not companies. It then dealt with the case of being sued in a representative capacity, where the same factors apply as applied in the part of the form dealing with a plaintiff suing in a representative capacity.

Then it dealt with partners, firms and businesses which are not limited companies. It said: 'If copartners are sued in the name of their firm, or a person carrying on business in a name other than his own name is sued in such name, add "(Sued as Firm)".' Emma had explored all the possibilities about getting the name right, and in her case it was a limited company. Where you sue a person or partners carrying on a business which is not a limited company, it is best to sue them in the name in which they carry on the business: 'Shocking Electrics' or 'Alipha

Typewriter Service Co'. The only thing is that you
have to add, as the form of request points out, the
words '(Sued as a firm)'.

Lastly in the panel of the form devoted to the
defendant's particulars was a requirement which directly applied to Emma's case. It said this: 'If a company registered under the Companies Act, 1948, is
sued, the address given must be the registered office
of the company, and must be so described'. Emma
completed the particulars of her defendant in this
way: 'Watsons Stores (Minford) Limited whose registered office is at 148 Buckingham Street, Guildford,
Surrey'.

If you are suing a defendant whose registered office
is in the district for the court or who resides in the
district, the form ends here. But in cases where the
defendant is outside the district for the court in which
the case is being brought, the form is longer. Emma
had to tackle the questions designed to make sure that
the local court could handle the case. There are
elaborate directions about which questions have to be
answered, and which do not. In fact for
straightforward cases, like Emma's, it was quite
simple. Only questions 1 and 2 had to be answered,
and this was easily done. '1. Was the purchase price
or rental payable in one sum?' Answer 'yes'. '2. Was
the contract made in the district of the court, and if
so, where?' Answer 'yes, at 12 High Street, Minford
Surrey'. By stating that it was at Minford that the
purchase of the goods had taken place, she showed
that her case could be brought in the Minford County
Court. And that was all that mattered.

All forms of request have at the bottom a place for the plaintiff to sign, and the form must be dated. There is also a further space to be completed which says: 'What the claim is for'. This merely requires a very brief description of the type of case it is. Emma wrote: 'Compensation for breach of contract'. In other cases, the sort of statement that might be filled in here could be: 'Price of goods sold', or 'damages for negligence' or 'possession of flat'.

The last item to be completed on the front of the form of request deals with money. It asks you to complete the 'Amount claimed'. In Emma's case this was not straightforward. Totting up the several money claims detailed in her particulars of claim, she arrived at the total of £96.90, made up from the refund of the purchase price (£84.50), and four items of out-of-pocket expenditure: launderette charges (£6), travelling expenses (£1), phone calls (40p) and damage to the kitchen floor (£5). To this had to be added the compensation for loss of use of the washing machine, and inconvenience—for this she was claiming general damages, with no precise sum as yet known. She had, however, limited her claim under this heading to £50. So adding the £50 to the £96.90, Emma put as the amount she claimed: £146.90.

court fees

Then the form asked her to complete: 'Fee on entering plaint'. This meant the court fee she had to pay in order to start her case. The amount of the fee depends on the amount claimed.

The court fees are as follows:

amount claimed	court fee
	£
not exceeding £10	1.00
over £10 to £20	2.50
„ £20 to £50	4.00
„ £50 to £100	5·00
„ £100 to £250	6.00
„ £250 to £500	7.00
„ £500	8.00

As Emma's claim was for £146.90, the court fee—
often referred to as the plaint fee—was £6. She
noticed that she could have increased the limit of her
claim for general damages without in fact having to
pay any more by way of plaint fee. The court fee of
£6 applied to all cases where the amount claimed was
between £100 and £250, so that she could take the
total of her claim up to £250 without increasing the
amount of the court fee she would have to pay. When
she noticed this, she decided to change the last item
in her particulars of claim to take account of this,
increasing the limit on the compensation claim to
£100. She did not really think that she would get
anything like as much as £100 for this and even £50
was pushing it a bit. But this was not a statement of
what in fact she thought she ought to get, but rather a
statement of the top limit of her claim, just for the
purpose of calculating the fee. On this basis, there
was no harm in raising the limit from £50 to £100,
just in case the judge was more than normally sympa-

thetic towards her claim and awarded her say, £75 compensation for a raw deal. The total of her claim now came to £196.90. She altered the 'Amount Claimed' to this figure, and entered £6 as the 'Fee on entering plaint'. (She made a corresponding alteration at the end of her particulars of claim, and initialled it.) She did not, however, make it more than £200 because if she were to lose her case, and costs were awarded against her, she could face a higher bill to pay. A higher scale of costs applies above £200.

Beneath that was a space for 'Solicitor's costs'. These are the fixed costs which the defendant has to pay as a contribution towards the costs of the plaintiff's solicitor, if he pays the debt claimed as soon as the summons is served. As Emma was not employing a solicitor, she could not claim anything for solicitors's costs. From January 1976, a plaintiff who does not employ a solicitor will, in some cases, be able to get something for the time and effort devoted to getting the case started in the county court.

That dealt with the form of request. There was a certificate on the back dealing with the question of serving the summons, that is, sending the summons to the defendant, so that the court could be sure he receives it and can thus be compelled to respond to it. If you are suing a limited company, the court serves the summons by sending it to the address where it is known the company can be found: the address of the registered office. When this happens, as in Emma's case, there is no fee for service. But if you are suing an individual or a firm which is not a limited company, you can serve the summons in person, yourself, by physically handing it to the defendant, but it is usual these days to get the court bailiff to do so. This costs an extra 75p, so that if Emma had been suing an individual, and getting the court to serve the summons, she would have had to pay an extra 75p fee on issuing the summons. Alternatively, if you are suing an individual or a firm which is not a limited company, you can ask the court to serve the summons by post. It is only where this is to happen that it is necessary for the plaintiff to complete the certificate about this on the back of the form of request.

plaint note

Now Emma had to pay the court fee for issuing the summons. Although county courts may accept cheques, Emma had brought the necessary cash with her. She took £6 out of her handbag. She caught the eye of the clerk, who had wandered away to leave her to her form-filling. She handed to him the completed form of request, the two copies of her particulars of claim and £6 in notes. He studied the forms carefully. All seemed to be in order. He then completed a form called a plaint note. This was partly a receipt for her £6 and partly her official identification for court purposes, and would have to be produced by her whenever she attended the court office for any step connected with her case. It was her identity card for the court officials. Emma put it into her file for safe keeping. The plaint note stated the plaint number— the reference number for the case which the court would always use. In her case it was 73/00534. She wrote this number on her copy of the particulars of claim, on the right-hand side at the top, in the space provided for this number. The clerk had done the same thing on the two copies he had taken away.

The plaint note revealed one other important matter. This was the date of the hearing that would take place in a few weeks time: the pre-trial review. This would be the occasion when, if Watsons wished to challenge her claim, they would appear with her before the registrar of the court, for him to consider what he could do to secure 'the just, expeditious and economical disposal' of the case.

'Is that all?' she asked of the clerk.

'That's all you have to do today,' he replied. 'The summons will be sent to the defendant within the next few days. We will let you know if we hear from them, although being a company I dare say they will contact you anyway, when they get the summons.'

Now she had to sit back and wait for something to happen. When Watsons received the summons, she would find out whether they would take any more notice of it than they had done of her letter before action.

A county court case may finish at any time. It is open to the parties to negotiate a settlement whenever and in whatever way they choose.

For a shop or other business, it can be very expensive to become involved in a contested court case. Even if they win, by the time they have paid their lawyers, and spent time in writing letters and having discussions about the details of the case, not to mention the time spent in court, it is hardly likely to have been worthwhile. The costs which the loser is ordered to pay may seem pretty hefty, but they do not as a rule cover anything like the full amount the winner actually has to expend. There may be the threat of publicity. No shop likes the prospect of reading in the local press a saga of a dissatisfied consumer, as described in court, whatever the outcome.

So strong are these pressures on shops, finance companies and other traders to avoid a court case, that some make it their policy never to fight one, but always to give way, believing that it is not worth it in the long run. You may find, therefore, that as soon as you embark seriously on disputing a case, you have won it. This, of course, is more likely to happen if your case has real merit. Shops have principles, too, and they may fight a case just to thwart somebody trying it on.

settling out of court
Of the large number of court cases that are started, comparatively few ever come to trial. Many are so clear-cut that they can hardly be argued about. If there is, in effect, no legal basis for a defence to your

claim, you may find that the service of a county court summons will end the matter swiftly, without argument or explanation. For one thing, it may get the shop (or whoever it is) to obtain legal advice for the first time on the matter, and this in itself could result in immediate settlement of your claim. Many shops do not understand or recognise their obligations under the Sale of Goods Act, for instance.

Some cases drag on longer. The defendants may put in a spirited defence, denying everything, and showing every sign of fighting the case vigorously to the bitter end. But then, as time goes by, they start to get fed up with the case. Solicitors ask for more details of this and that, and more time and money seems to be required to continue the contest, and after a while they try to settle the case. They may, for instance, pay part of what you claim, while disputing the rest of it. You then have to decide whether to accept what they pay, and abandon the rest, or hold out for what you are actually claiming.

There can be an important question of costs that arises in these circumstances. Suppose you are claiming £150 damages from your garage alleging faulty servicing. They dispute that it was faulty, and say that even if it was, your claim is exaggerated. They pay £95 into court, that is, lodge that sum with the court office, and indicate that they think that is all you would get if you won. You are then in a dilemma: if you go on with the case, spurning the implied offer to settle at £95, win it and are awarded the whole of your claim of £150 (or any amount higher than what has been paid into court), you will also recover the greater part of your legal costs. The more you are awarded, the higher the costs that you will recover. If, however, you go on with the case and in the end are awarded only something up to £95, you will be ordered to pay the garage's legal costs incurred from the time they paid the £95 into court, as well as having to pay your own. Yours would be an empty victory, in fact, because the chances are that the whole of the damages you get would be eaten up in paying their costs. So you have to weigh things up very carefully in deciding whether to accept the £95 they paid into court, or go on for the £150 you are claiming. The judge never knows if a defendant has paid a sum into court, or how much, until after he has given judgment.

It is always best to settle a case, if you possibly can. If in doubt, compromise. It is usually wise to accept any reasonable offer to drop the case. You may sue for £100, they may pay £40 into court and write to you, offering to make it £50 for a quick settlement. After laughing off their advances, you may counter with an offer to settle for £80, whereupon they go to their 'last offer' of £60 and you end up settling for £70. There is nothing dishonourable about such a settlement. And you can—if you are good at that sort of thing—indulge in a certain amount of brinkmanship in the process. You may stoutly deny any intention of settling for a penny less than your claim, but by keeping open your options, you may be able to jack up their offer by another £10 or so, in the end.

Negotiations intended to lead to a settlement are

best conducted behind a veil derived from the expression 'without prejudice'. If the negotiations break down so that, after all, the case has to end in a trial before a judge, neither side would wish to disclose to the court the details of the negotiations. Awkward questions might be asked in court about what led to the negotiations, and about matters discussed in them. To avoid any embarrassment of that kind, therefore, negotiations with a view to a settlement are usually expressly dubbed 'without prejudice'. If these words appear at the top of any letters, or precede a conversation, neither side can refer to anything said in such letters or discussions, when the trial takes place.

When you reach agreement with the other side about a county court case on the basis that you are to be paid an agreed sum of money, make sure that the money is actually paid into court or that you get the actual money before you abandon the case. Only when you have the cash in your hands should you formally discontinue the court case. When your money, including any sum agreed to cover your costs, has been received by you, write to the registrar of the court explaining what has happened and stating that the action is settled. If the defendant has paid money into court, it is necessary to extract the sum out of court as part of the arrangement to settle the case. You must write to the court to say that you accept the settlement, enclosing a note signed by the defendant agreeing that the sum in court be taken out by you as part of the settlement.

Quite a few cases are settled in the corridor outside the court room, just as the trial is about to begin.

Some are settled even after the trial has begun, during an adjournment, for instance. It is never too late to settle. When considering a settlement, it is important to look at the whole of the case realistically and objectively. It is easy to become so convinced of the justice of your cause that you cannot see the possibility of your losing. Or you may be absolutely determined not to let the defendant get away with anything at all, just to show him. This is mistaken thinking. Your whole strategy should be directed towards getting a settlement, if at all possible. If you have included one or two arguable items in your particulars of claim, when a settlement comes into the offing, you may have something to give away in the negotiations. Inevitably, a settlement means that each side makes some concessions.

The sooner you tell a court office about a settlement, the better, as they assume, unless they hear to the contrary, that the case is going on. They compile the list of cases for hearing on particular days on the assumption that each case is still to be fought. It is understandably maddening for them to find cases they have listed which are not to be fought after all, because they have been settled.

And so it might have been in Emma's case. As soon as Watsons were served with the summons, they might immediately have made a payment into court of the sum claimed for the price of the washing machine. It is surprising, really, that they did not do this. If this had happened, Emma would have had to consider carefully what she would do about the other items on her claim. She would not be likely to have totally abandoned the rest of her claim, but she might well have held out for a few more pounds—the £12.40 say, for her out of pocket expenses—at the same time abandoning her claim for compensation for inconvenience and disappointment.

further particulars
Just over a week after she had issued the summons, Emma received a letter from Watson's solicitors. This is what they said:

> *1 Charter Street,*
> *Minford, Surrey.*
> *19th January 1973*

Dear Sirs

> *Watsons Stores (Minford) Limited ats Yourself*

We are instructed by Messrs Watsons Stores (Minford) Limited, who have handed to us the county court summons you have issued and which has been served upon them. Kindly note that we are acting for them in connection with these proceedings.

Our clients have a complete defence to your claim, and these proceedings are, according to our instructions, wholly misconceived. We shall be filing a defence shortly, but in the meantime please confirm that you will extend our time for filing defence.

We enclose a request for further and better particulars of your claim, service of which please acknowledge. We would point out that we are entitled to require you to provide the particulars requested. If you intend to instruct solicitors in this matter, we suggest that you hand the enclosed notice to whichever firm you instruct.

> *Yours faithfully*
> *DODDS & SON*

Mrs. Emma Seaton.

The heading of the letter spoke of Watsons 'ats Yourself'. Ats stands for the 'at the suit of', meaning 'being sued by'. They might well have described the case like a football match, that is, as Watsons v Yourself. The point of ats is to indicate which side the solicitors represent. The custom is that a solicitor, in describing a court case, names his own client first. Thus a solicitor acting for a defendant uses 'ats', putting his client's name first (Bloggs ats Jones). A solicitor acting for a plaintiff says 'Jones v Bloggs', again putting his client's name first.

It is common for solicitors to declare unflinching faith in their client's cause, without much regard to the merits at first sight. It is their job to support their clients, so the first thing they do is to assert that the client's case is irrefutable. Among the profession to assert or respond to a claim with anything less may be considered a sign of weakness.

At this stage, Emma was not in the least put off by the brisk confidence expressed in the letter. The assertion that her claim was wholly misconceived (a common legal cliché) was, she knew, quite wrong. It is true, of course, that many shops do think that claims against them by the unfortunate buyers of faulty goods are misconceived, because they do not recognise the nature and the extent of their legal responsibilities.

The solicitors asked for more time for filing their defence. This was fair enough. By law there is a time limit of 14 days from the day when the summons is served, taking that day as the first day, for the defendant to prepare and deliver the document setting out his grounds for disputing the case: the defence. If Emma were to refuse extra time, the solicitors could apply to the registrar of the court for an extension, and if they did, an extension would almost certainly be granted. In view of this, there was little point in refusing more time.

Enclosed with this letter was a formidable looking document called a request for further and better particulars of claim. All it amounted to really was a request that Emma should state in a little more detail certain matters which she had already set out in her particulars of claim. It was, however, wrapped up in a strange legal way, so that it was rather daunting at first sight. This is how it read:

IN THE MINFORD COUNTY COURT

Plaint No: 73/00534

Between

Emma Caroline Seaton (Married Woman)   *Plaintiff*
          and
Watsons Stores (Minford) Limited   *Defendant*

Request For Further and Better Particulars of Particulars of Claim

1. Under paragraph 3 of the Particulars of Claim, of the allegation that the washing machine referred to in paragraph 1 of the said particulars broke down, specifying the manner in which the said machine is alleged to have broken down, and of the cause thereof; and of the alleged defect in the mechanism of the said machine, specifying the nature of the said defect, and of the part of the said mechanism alleged to be defective.

2. Under paragraph 6 of the Particulars of Claim, of the allegation that the said machine broke down again, specify-

ing the manner in which the said machine is alleged to have broken down again, and of the cause thereof; and the alleged rumbling noise in the said machine, specifying the nature and the cause of the said noise.

3. Under paragraph 7 of the Particulars of Claim, of the allegation that the said machine did not seem to deal with the washing as well as it had done stating in what respects it did not do so; and of the allegation that the said machine broke down a third time, and the cause thereof, and of the alleged inability to pump out water, specifying the nature and the cause of the alleged inability.

4. Under paragraph 8 of the Particulars of Claim, of the allegation that the said machine broke down yet again; specifying the nature and the cause of the said further breakdown, and of the alleged failure of the connection carrying the water which became dislodged, specifying which connection, and how it became dislodged.

Dated the 19th day of January 1973

To the Plaintiff   Dodds & Son,
                                          1 Charter Street,
                                          Minford, Surrey
                           Solicitors for the Defendant.

All they wanted really was more information about what Emma said went wrong with her washing machine. But in asking for 'further and better particulars', they adopted the formal language that lawyers sometimes use for this exercise. They could have asked for these extra details by letter. Emma suspected that part at least of the reason for chucking this lot at her was to try and put her off her stroke in bringing the case, to make her puzzled and frightened, and as a result perhaps abandon her claim. If so, they were unlucky.

A request for further and better particulars can be something of a manoeuvre. One side seeks a tactical advantage by drawing the other side to commit himself to a particular line on matters in dispute, and so prevent the case being left general and unspecific. So far as it is possible, it is better not to elaborate on your claim with too much detail, if you can avoid it. There have been cases where one side is outflanked by his opponent partly because of the additional particulars he gives about aspects of his claim.

There is no exact rule about how much each side has to state. The other side is entitled to know in advance what case he or she has to meet, but not more than that. It does not follow, just because your opponent asks for 'further and better particulars' that you are bound to give them. You do not have to reveal details of the evidence you intend to produce to prove your case, for example.

Applying her mind to the tortuous language used, Emma came to realise that what they were saying, in each paragraph of their document, was: please give us more information of various statements in your particulars of claim. In paragraph 1 where you say the washing machine broke down, tell us how it broke down, and why; and when you say that there was a defect in the mechanism, tell us more about the defect, and exactly which part was causing the trouble. And so on. To make sense of the wording of the document, she had to interpose each time 'please give us further and better particulars'.

Emma was in a bit of a difficulty here. She really did not know what was wrong with the machine. She was no expert. The person who might be able to provide the details was the mechanic from the manufacturer, Toltons, who had come to fix the machine, each time it had broken down. Emma had not yet heard from Toltons in response to her original letter telling them about her proposed action against Watsons. If she were at this stage to try to extract this information in order to give the information requested by Dodds & Son, she would probably not get very far. She might eventually have to require the mechanic from Toltons to come to the trial of her case to give evidence. If she obtained a witness summons from the court and served it on the mechanic (as she intended to, if she had to), he would have no option but to come to court for this purpose. But what could she do now? She decided that she would write to Toltons once again, put them in the picture, and endeavour to obtain more information about the cause of the breakdowns. Then she could tell Dodds & Son, and the registrar if need be, that she had done her best to get the further particulars they had asked for.

This is the letter she wrote to Toltons:

14 Twintree Avenue
Minford, Surrey
24 January 1973

Dear Sirs,

I wrote to you on 11 December 1972 about the trouble I have been having with my Washfaster washing machine, and told you that I had cancelled my purchase of it from the shop where I bought it, Watsons in Minford, and was demanding my money back, plus compensation. Watsons have refused this, so I am now suing them in the Minford county court. For this purpose, I need details from you of the faults found in the machine by the mechanic from your company who came to my house to repair the machine.

The solicitors acting for Watsons have required me to provide them with exact particulars of the faults found in the machine on the occasion of each visit by your mechanic, including 'the nature of the said defect and of the part of the said mechanism alleged to be defective'.

The three visits about which I seek information were made by your man in June, August and October 1972. I do not have the exact dates. Your service department's records will no doubt show the name of the mechanic who did the work on each occasion, and details of the faults found, and work done. I shall be glad if you will let me have this information as soon as possible.

When, in due course, this case is heard in court, it will be necessary for me to ask your mechanic to come to court to give evidence about what he found wrong with the washing machine, and about what he did to put it right. I would like to know at this stage, therefore, whether you and he are willing that he should do this. If not, I shall have to apply for a witness summons from the court, requiring his attendance there. Perhaps you would let me know this, and at the same time inform me of his full name and address.

Yours faithfully,
Emma Seaton

Toltons Domestic Appliances Ltd.
S.E. Area Servicing Depot,
349 Godalming Road,
Guildford, Surrey.

This letter served a triple purpose in forwarding Emma's case. Firstly, it sought to obtain some information about the technical details of the faults in the washing machine. For this she could have called in a new expert herself, but she wished to avoid this step if possible, due to the expense it would involve. Secondly, it gave Toltons advance warning to have their mechanic ready to give evidence for her, when the case was heard at some time in the future. It is always worth giving plenty of notice to potential witnesses, as they may be hard to get if you delay.

Thirdly, the letter to Toltons showed them, too, that Emma really meant business. Toltons had shrugged off Emma's genuine and deeply felt complaints, much as Watsons had done. Now the shrugging had to stop. Watsons might have already made some approach to Toltons about her case. But if so she had not been told about this. The receipt of this letter would probably spur some sort of action out of Toltons.

On the same day, Emma wrote an acknowledgment to Dodds & Son:

14 Twintree Avenue
Minford, Surrey
24 January 1973

Dear Sirs,

Myself v Watsons

Thank you for your letter. By all means defer filing the defence for the time being. I extend your time by 7 days at this stage. If you need a further extension, please let me know, and I will consider it sympathetically.

You will appreciate that I am not an engineer and do not have details of what caused the machine to go wrong so often and so drastically. I am doing what I can to

obtain the information you have asked for, and if it comes
to hand, I will let you have it.

Yours faithfully,
Emma Seaton

Dodds & Son
1 Charter Street,
Minford, Surrey.

Emma gave Dodds & Son an extension of 7 days
only, telling them that they might get more. In that
time she hoped to hear from Toltons, and would
know what particulars she could provide about the
cause of the breakdowns of the washing machine. She
could then consider what information she could send
to Dodds & Son, to meet with their request. A
defendant has to deliver his defence, even though he
has asked for further particulars and not received
them.

Emma had issued the summons on 11 January
1973. She had been informed that the hearing of the
pre-trial review by the registrar would be on 20 February 1973. At the present rate of progress there
seemed every reason to think that this time-table
would fit in well with the unfolding of events. If
Toltons took an undue time to reply to her letter, or
if there were other causes of delay on either side, it
could be that by the date fixed for the hearing of the
pre-trial review, not much progress would have been
made. Nevertheless, the hearing date would stand, the
registrar would then consider the state of things as
they then stood, and make decisions about procedure
for the rest of the case, up to the actual trial. Emma
hoped that by the time the hearing of the pre-trial

review took place, she would have received the defence from Dodds & Son, setting out their answer to her claim in detail. If not, the registrar would, at the pre-trial review, almost certainly give directions about when they should deliver their defence, as well as other procedural matters.

Meanwhile, the washing machine still sat uselessly in the kitchen. Emma and Matthew decided that this was no longer acceptable. With the help of a neighbour, they removed it to the garage, where it was not so much in the way. Technically, as Emma had already cancelled her purchase due to the defects, the washing machine belonged to Watsons once again. But it was still in Emma's possession, and she was legally bound to take good care of it. She was not entitled to dump it, or leave it in the open air to deteriorate. She decided that the time had come to buy another washing machine, and did so.

Emma received a reply from Toltons. This is what it said:

> *Toltons Domestic Appliances Ltd.*
> *S.E. Area Servicing Depot,*
> *349 Godalming Road,*
> *Guildford, Surrey.*
> *31st January 1973*

Dear Madam,

We have duly received your letter and are sorry to hear that you are experiencing difficulties with your Washfaster Machine. We note with great surprise the steps that you have taken in this matter, and much regret that you felt it necessary to go to these lengths in order to resolve your problems. Our service engineer who called at your premises is Mr. David Richardson, but we cannot at this stage give

*you any details of his findings when visiting you to adjust
your machine, nor of the work he carried out. We note that
you propose to ask him to support your case, but cannot
comment further on your plans in this connection. We are
getting in touch with Messrs Watsons Stores (Minford)
Ltd on this matter, and would express the hope that this
unfortunate business can be resolved quickly and without
further unpleasantness.*

Yours faithfully,
M. G. Bugden,
Service Manager

Mrs. E. Seaton.

In effect, they were still shrugging off their responsibilities, although some little progress had been
made. At least she knew the name of the man to call
to give evidence. As to finding out details of the cause
of the breakdowns in the machine, Emma was no further forward. Toltons had managed to sidestep her
request for information about this. She therefore
wrote to Dodds & Son, saying this:

14 Twintree Avenue,
Minford, Surrey.
4 February 1973

Dear Sirs,

Myself v Watsons

*I have now heard from Toltons, the manufacturers who
repaired my washing machine every time it broke down.
They have failed to give me details of their findings, or of
the work they carried out. I cannot therefore provide you
with the greater part of the particulars you asked for in
your request dated 19 January. In any case, I do not consider that you are entitled to them.*

The only particulars requested which I can provide are under para 3 of your request, where you ask for particulars of my allegation that 'the said machine did not seem to deal with the washing as well as it had done'. The particulars of that matter are as follows:

> *'When the machine broke down in August 1972, it was repaired by the mechanic from Toltons (the manufacturer) for the second time. After that, I found that, although the machine went through the cycle of operations it was intended to follow, it did not in fact wash the clothes so effectively as it had done immediately before the most recent breakdown. I also found that it did not spin the clothes so well, more water being retained in the clothes than before. It seemed that the machine lacked power after that repair.'*

The time for delivering defence, allowing for the 7-day extension I granted to you, expires next week and I take it that you will now be able to meet this time limit.

> *Yours faithfully*
> *Emma Seaton*

Dodds & Son.

defence

Emma thus responded to Dodds & Son's salvo in which they had demanded further and better particulars of her claim. She had given them only a fraction of what they had asked for, and what she had given them was not much more than a gesture. If they thought they were entitled to more information, they would no doubt ask the registrar of the court to order Emma to provide it at the hearing of the pre-trial review in a week or two's time. The chances were, in fact, that they would not pursue the question further.

And so it turned out. Just over a week later, Emma

heard from Dodds & Son:

> *1 Charter Street,*
> *Minford, Surrey.*
> *12th February 1973*

Dear Madam,

> *Watsons Stores (Minford) Ltd ats Yourself*

We thank you for your letter of 4th February and have noted the contents. We do not accept that our clients are not entitled to the particulars requested, but in the circumstances do not propose to pursue the matter further.

We now enclose a copy of our clients' defence, which we have today filed with the registrar of the Minford County Court. Please accept service by post and acknowledge.

> *Yours faithfully*
> *Dodds & Son*

Mrs. Emma Seaton.

The last sentence was a formality. Emma had given at the very end of her particulars of claim, her 'address for service', that is, the address where all the documents connected with the case were to be sent to. In her case, naturally it was to her own home address. If she had been represented by a solicitor, it would have been his address. Having given an address for service, it went without saying that the defence would be sent to her at that address. All the same they used the phrase about 'accepting service by post'. To ask Emma to acknowledge safe receipt of the defence was fair enough.

This is how the defence was worded:

IN THE MINFORD COUNTY COURT
                                    Plaint No: 73/00534

Between

Emma Caroline Seaton (Married Woman)   *Plaintiff*
        and

Watsons Stores (Minford) Limited   *Defendant*

DEFENCE

1. Paragraphs 1 and 2 of the Particulars of Claim are admitted.

2. Paragraphs 3 to 10 inclusive of the Particulars of Claim are not admitted.

3. Save and except that it is admitted that the Plaintiff by letter dated 11th December 1972 wrote to the Defendant purporting to cancel the purchase of the washing machine referred to in the Particulars of Claim, and that the Defendant by letter of 14th December 1972 replied thereto, the Defendant does not admit paragraphs 11 and 12 of the Particulars of Claim. The Defendant will refer at the trial to the said letters for their full content and effect.

4. Paragraph 13 of the Particulars of Claim is denied.

5. If (which is not admitted) the said washing machine was defective, the defects were not such as to render it unfit for its intended purpose, or of unmerchantable quality. Further, or in the alternative, the alleged defects were of a minor character and readily capable of correction by adjustment or servicing under the terms of the guarantee of the said machine provided by the manufacturers therof. Further or in the alternative, the alleged defects were due to the manner in which the said machine had been used since the time it was delivered by the Defendant to the Plaintiff.

6. Paragraph 14 of the Particulars of Claim is not admitted.

7. Save as hereinbefore expressly admitted, the Defendant denies each and every allegation of fact contained in the Particulars of Claim.

KEITH SANDERS

Dated 12th February 1973

To the Registrar of the Court and to the Plaintiff

Dodds & Son
1 Charter Street, Minford, Surrey,
Solicitors for the Defendant,
who will accept service
of all proceedings on their behalf
at the said address.

The name that appeared at the end of the text was the name of the barrister who had drawn up the defence. (If no name appears there, the defence has been drawn up by the solicitors.) This showed that Dodds & Son had taken counsel's opinion, that is the opinion of a barrister, on the case, and instructed him to prepare the defence. Emma could now expect to find herself pitted against counsel, when her case came to trial.

The purpose of the defence is to set out the basis on which the defendant challenges the plaintiff's claim. The defendant may do this in a number of ways. He may say: 'I do not agree that any of what you say happened'. Or he may say: 'I agree with some of what you say happened, but not with the rest'. The defendant may say instead: 'I agree with what you say happened, but I say that it does not make me legally liable for what you claim'. Or he may even say: 'I do not agree with what you say. But even if I did, I say that it does not make me legally liable for what you claim'.

The defence may then go on to admit or to deny that the plaintiff actually incurred the expenses, and other items of loss or damage, set out in the particulars of claim. Or the defence may say that even if they were incurred, they did not directly result from the alleged happenings. There are many possible variations in how the defence may go about disclaiming liability.

Allegations of fact in the particulars of claim may, in the defence, be admitted, or not admitted, or denied. If a fact is admitted, the plaintiff does not, at the trial of the case, have to produce any evidence of it. The defendant's admission counts as proof of it. If a fact is not admitted, in effect the defendant is saying: 'Well, that may be true, but I am not admitting it. If you want to rely on that fact as part of your case, you jolly well prove it'. If a fact is denied, in effect the defendant is saying: 'That's not true'. This may in effect, be saying 'You are a liar' or it may be saying 'You are mistaken' or it may mean 'You are a liar or mistaken or both'.

It is not always possible to say exactly what is fact and what is not. If you say: 'this pen does not write at all', that is obviously a statement of fact. What about 'this pen is not much good'; is that a statement of fact? And how about 'this pen is unfit for the purpose for which it was intended, and is not of merchantable quality'? In those cases questions of fact are obviously involved, but they are not pure questions of fact: questions of judgment, or qualitative assessments are also involved. They are what you might call secondary questions of fact, derived from primary questions of fact, such as: Does the pen write? Does it write clearly and smoothly? Is it scratchy or rough? Is the line clean? Does it smudge? and so on.

The defence in a court case sometimes agrees with some of the primary facts while challenging some of the secondary facts, or conclusions, alleged to be derived from them. Thus you often find that court cases are deeply concerned with questions of cause and effect, and whether a combination of facts amounts to some overall legally defined concept: for instance, reasonableness or fitness for purpose, or merchantable quality, or compliance with description, or negligence.

Emma now had a good idea what the contest would be all about. All that Watsons accepted, in effect, was that she bought the washing machine from them and that she wrote to them purporting to cancel the purchase. They did not accept that it went wrong as she alleged, or that she was entitled to anything at all. They several times used the legal cliché: 'Further or in the alternative . . .'. This meant to say: 'Here is an additional point about what we have just said, or—in case it really turns out to be a separate point altogether—an alternative justification for what we are saying'. It is the lawyers' version of the story of the boy and the broken window, who said 'It is not broken. If it is, I didn't do it. If I did it, it was an accident.'

Emma now knew that she was going to have to prove what went wrong with the machine. The main way of doing this would be her own evidence, that is, what she herself would say to the judge in the court on oath when the case came to trial. Some people overlook the simple fact that their own story is often the most valuable piece of evidence they have. 'But I have no proof. It is just my word against theirs' they complain and contemplate dropping their case. It is better to have someone to back up your evidence, preferably someone who is independent, but your own words count.

Emma could now see that it would certainly be necessary for her to call as a witness the man from Toltons who fixed the washing machine when it went wrong. The only other evidence she was likely to require would be that of her husband, to confirm what she said about the machine having gone wrong.

If the defence had not given sufficient details of the facts Watsons sought to rely on, Emma could now call on them to supply further and better particulars of the defence, just as they had sought to obtain further and better particulars of her claim. She would merely have written a letter to Dodds & Son, asking for the particulars she needed, referring to the paragraphs and the particular statements in the defence which she required to be amplified. It would not have been necessary for her to do what they had done, that is, to prepare a formal document called a request for further and better particulars, although she could have done that, if she had preferred. If they had refused to provide the particulars she had asked for, or if the particulars they supplied had not been sufficient, she would have been able to raise the matter at the pre-trial review.

In the event, Emma did not need any further and

better particulars of the defence. In effect, Watsons were not alleging any new facts in their defence. They were merely not accepting the facts (and the conclusions from those facts) which Emma was putting forward in her claim.

So, pleadings were now closed, as lawyers say. This means that the parties have set on paper, and given to the court and to each other, the essential details of their case in the form of particulars of claim and defence, and any further particulars.

thinking about discovery
There was now little more to do until the pre-trial review. At the pre-trial review, the registrar would go into the questions at issue, and make certain rulings about procedures.

One matter which would probably arise for consideration was the procedure for each side looking at, and obtaining copies of, the other side's documents. The process of revealing to the other side documents connected with a case is called discovery of documents, and sometimes forms an important part of getting at the truth of a case. Emma would have the right to see any relevant documents Watsons had about the case. Emma considered carefully what useful information she might be able to unearth by requiring Watsons to reveal their documents. At first sight there did not seem to be much. She could, however, find out what Watsons had written to Toltons, and anyone else, about her complaint, from the time when she started writing awkward letters to them. She could delve into their books, and stock records, and perhaps discover when they had taken the machine into stock, what profit they had made on it, and so on. There did not seem to be much point in that, but you never know. There is always just the chance that you might stumble on some little fact, which, on closer examination, sheds a great deal of light.

Mulling it over in her mind, Emma decided she would at least ask for discovery of Watsons' records regarding the washing machine. The point of her thinking about this now, instead of later on, when discovery was actually due, was this. Discovery would come up at the pre-trial review. The registrar would perhaps say: 'Do you want discovery in this case?' It would be too late then to start thinking about it.

Few people realise the importance of discovery. Fewer still appreciate the dangers of it. Because you must reveal any relevant documents to the other side, you can easily damage your own case, or make yourself look stupid, by having to disclose documents that you have in your possession relating to your case. In fact, it is a good idea to remember the implications of discovery right from the outset of any dispute, and even before, if that is possible. A careful person realises that almost any bit of paper which he writes upon or which comes his way may one day be revealed to an opponent, and gazed at with care by a court deciding a vital issue in a case. Take, for instance, letters. Some people write remarks on them in ink or ball point pen. This is a bad idea. If you want to make notes about original documents, make them on separate bits of paper which can be kept or thrown away, separately, if need be. You might look very silly in court trying to explain why certain words are written in ink alongside one paragraph of a letter from your opponent, when you produce the original letter in court. You cannot get round a problem like that by making a copy of the letter, leaving out the comment you made, because originals must always be produced, if they still exist.

The same thinking should apply to letters, and other documents, which you write to other people about the matter in dispute. Any letter is likely to be revealed to the other side, and to the court, as a result of discovery of documents. You are not allowed to suppress evidence, just because it hinders your case. You have to reveal all. The main exceptions are letters to and from your solicitor, and notes and memoranda you prepare for your own purposes (aide-memoires, draft letters and such like).

you have to reveal all . . . .

If Emma had had any misgivings about her prospects of winning her case, now would have been a good time to think about abandoning it. The other side would very soon be incurring quite a lot of expense with legal fees, and if she were to delay abandoning her case until later on, she would by then have much bigger legal costs to meet. The rule is that if you abandon your case, you have to pay your opponent's costs right up to the time you abandon it. So it is always worthwhile abandoning sooner, rather than later, if you have to abandon the case at all. It is also worthwhile going through the papers in the case, carefully, from the beginning, every so often, just to give yourself a chance of seeing if the case still stands up, in the light of the most recent developments.

It is easy to lose sight of things which happened in the earlier stages, or to overlook their importance in the light of later revelations, after the case has been going for some time. Taking stock every so often is a very good idea. This is what Emma did at this stage in her case, just as she was approaching the pre-trial review.

The plaint note handed to Emma by the clerk at the county court when she had issued the summons had told her of the date fixed for the hearing of the pre-trial review. It was due to take place at the court at 10.30 am on 20 February 1973. If that date had not been convenient to either side, they could have asked the court for an adjournment to another day.

On the morning of that day, she took all her papers in connection with the case, whether she thought they would be needed or not, and arrived at the court building in good time. Inside the building, she found a list pinned up outside one of the courts, giving the names of the cases to be considered that morning. There were between thirty and forty of them, not all of which were pre-trial reviews. Half-way down the list she found 'Seaton v Watsons Stores (Minford) Ltd'. She cautiously poked her head round the door of the court, to find a few people sitting and standing around the court room, waiting for the session to begin. The registrar had not yet arrived, but a man she took to be a court clerk was standing by the front of the court, going through some papers. She went up to him. 'Excuse me,' she said 'can you tell me please if this is the right place for my case?' She produced her plaint note, and indicated the time and date on it. 'I am Emma Seaton,' she added 'the plaintiff, and I do not have a solicitor.'

'Yes, this is the place. Your case won't be on for some time. The registrar will be here in a moment to start his list,' he said. 'Just one more thing,' said Emma 'Do you happen to know if anyone from Dodds & Son is here? They represent the other side in my case.' 'Dodds & Son,' replied the clerk, recognising the name, 'Lets have a look? No, I don't see anyone from them here yet. But I dare say they'll arrive before long.' Emma retreated to the back of the court and sat down. In some county courts, pre-trial reviews are held in the registrar's room, not in a courtroom. People waiting for their case to be heard, wait outside.

Emma went through the papers in her case, but could not concentrate on them. Outside the door of the courtroom she heard names being shouted from time to time. Suddenly she heard her own name—'Seaton'— which made her jump. She dashed out, to find a young man calling her name. He was from Dodds & Son. It is quite usual for each side to identify the other outside a courtroom by calling out the name of a firm or person wanted, and just wait for someone to appear. Emma introduced herself. He said he was an articled clerk, that is, an apprentice solicitor, and seemed to be quite charming. His name was Leslie Coales. 'Do you know what is supposed to be happening this morning?' Emma asked.

'Well,' he said, 'I have not done many of these pre-trial things before, as a matter of fact. But as a rule the old registrar just asks what we want to organise about the trial, and all that stuff. There's nothing to it really. I don't see the point of this new procedure, quite honestly.'

'Well, from my point of view, it's a godsend,' said Emma. 'It gives me a chance to make sure I've got it right so far.'

They chatted for a while about the technicalities of

the case. 'He'll ask us about discovery, presumably,' said Emma, putting on a knowing air. The young man looked a bit surprised at the way she trotted out the jargon.

After talking for a while, they quietly slipped into the court room. By this time, the registrar had begun the hearing of the cases on his morning list. The court was sitting in chambers, that is to say, the court was not officially open to the public although there seemed to be nobody there to stop the public wandering in, if they wanted to. Some registrars are very strict about hearings in chambers and do not allow any outsider to be present at a pre-trial review.

It was hardly possible for Emma to hear what the registrar was saying to those concerned in the case currently being dealt with. The registrar, with his clerk, was sitting at the front of the court, and the two people involved in the hearing were sitting opposite him on the other side of the table. They were talking quietly, and only those with the most acute hearing could catch anything of what they were saying to each other. After a while, one hearing ended and another began, the clerk announcing the names of the parties as each hearing was about to begin. Then the people in the next case would come forward and take their place opposite the registrar.

A variety of applications was being heard. In one, a solicitor representing a defendant was asking for an order that the plaintiff should supply further particulars of his claim. In another, a debtor was asking for more time to pay a sum owed.

Very soon, the registrar started to hear pre-trial

reviews. There was a whole batch of them in which the plaintiff was the electricity board, and the sums being claimed were for electricity supply.

Emma was slightly surprised at the apparent informality of the proceedings, and by the fact that a pre-trial review, on average, did not last more than five minutes. She had to sit through quite a few cases before her turn was reached. It was nearly 11.30 am when the clerk called out 'Seaton and Watsons'.

hearing of the pre-trial review

Emma and the man from Dodds & Son walked to the front of the court, smiled weakly at the registrar and his clerk, murmured a vague 'Good morning, sir,' and sat down side by side at the table.

The registrar was not after all a crusty old lawyer, but a middle-aged man with a kind and sympathetic manner. 'You are Mrs. Seaton?' he asked Emma.

'That's right,' she said.

'And you are from Dodds & Son?' he asked of Emma's opponent.

'Yes, sir.'

'If you will excuse me I will just have a glance at these papers,' the registrar said. Emma noticed that he was reading through her particulars of claim, comparing it from time to time with the defence. He nodded his head gently, as if in understanding, now and again, and occasionally glanced up at Emma and her opponent. When he had gathered the gist of what the case was all about, he looked up and said: 'Yes. Well, this should be an interesting case. The pleadings seem clear enough to me. Mrs. Seaton, you are not represented by a solicitor, but you seem to have produced particulars of claim which are quite satisfactory. Do you wish to add anything to them, or amend them in any way? I sometimes find it helpful to suggest more clarification or additions to particulars of claim. But so far as I can see that is not necessary in your case. Do you agree?'

'Well, sir,' said Emma, 'I have nothing to add to what I have already stated there, thank you. If you think they are all in order, I am very happy to be guided by you.'

'Mr. Coales,' said the registrar, 'are you content with the state of the pleadings? Do you need any further particulars?'

'There was a stage,' said Mr. Coales, 'when we were asking for further and better particulars of the claim, but we are not pursuing that now. We are quite happy with the pleadings, sir, if you are.'

'I should explain, Mrs. Seaton,' said the registrar, 'that this is not, of course, the trial of your case. It is a preliminary consideration by me, to see if there is anything the court can do to assist the parties. Sometimes we can help them to reach agreement about things in dispute. We try to prepare the ground in order to make the trial of the case in due course as smooth, efficient and speedy as possible. In some cases, where the parties are not legally represented, for example, I can suggest ways in which they might express their claim a bit more clearly. Then there are cases where there is really no real dispute about the matter, because the claim is not challenged. For example, the defendant may just be short of money, and in those cases I can dispose of the case without more ado, and judgment could be entered, and I could make an order about how the debt is to be paid. In practice this happens quite often, and quite a few cases are finished at the pre-trial review.

'But of course, you have a contested case here, so my job is to help you, and the solicitor for the other side, to get as many matters agreed as possible at this stage, so as to narrow the differences that will be fought out at the trial, and to give any other directions and advice that I can, that will assist in disposing of this case as smoothly as possible.'

—arbitration

From October 1973, cases can be referred to arbitration instead of being tried in court. This means that the matter can be resolved more informally than at a trial in court, and costs can be considerably reduced. The registrar can order arbitration at the pre-trial review, and it is usually the registrar himself who will be the arbitrator.

Arbitration is generally intended for cases where not more than £100 is at stake, but can be used for bigger cases instead of trial, if both parties agree.

At an arbitration, witnesses and documents can still carry weight, and an understanding of presenting evidence can be of great value even where the rules and procedure are relaxed.

The decision of the arbitrator has the force of law, counts as a judgment and can be enforced by the county court.

—expert investigation and evidence

The registrar can, in suitable cases, appoint a referee. For instance, a technical question could be referred to an expert who would make an investigation and report his findings to the registrar. In such a case, it would be unnecessary for each side to call their own expert, and so costs could be reduced.

Technical matters are sometimes resolved by one of the parties having an expert prepare a report and if the report is satisfactory to both sides, they agree it. The report is then treated in court as agreed evidence, so that no expert on this particular matter needs to attend the trial.

The registrar continued: 'We ought perhaps to consider next the question of expert evidence, seeing that this case will go for trial in the usual way. I imagine much is going to turn on what engineers say about the state of the machinery inside Mrs. Seaton's washing machine, don't you? In which case, I think you ought to try to agree an expert's report. Failing this, we should limit the experts to, say one on each side. That's enough, isn't it? We don't want strings of professors and consultant engineers coming along for a case of this kind. Are you prepared to agree that, Mr. Coales?'

'I don't think we could oppose that, sir,' said the young man from Dodds & Son.

The registrar's placing a limit on how much expert evidence could be produced on each side would help Emma considerably. It meant that Watsons could not swamp her case by a mass of technicalities propounded by a succession of experts, something which Watsons—but not she—could afford to arrange. It meant that in this respect, at least, they could not gain an advantage over her by their stronger financial position.

'There is just one thing, however,' said Mr. Coales. 'The machine is still in Mrs. Seaton's possession. We would like an opportunity of having it inspected by our expert, if that is all right.'

'There's no problem about that, is there Mrs. Seaton?' said the registrar. 'You would not mind an engineer instructed by the defendants coming along to see the machine?'

'Not at all,' said Emma. 'It's in our garage. We've bought a different washing machine now, and we regard the old one as belonging to Watsons. It's their property and their responsibility, so of course they can come and look at it whenever they like. They can take it away, too, if they want. Although, on second thoughts, perhaps it had better stay where it is until this case is over. It is my chief item of evidence, and I ought to protect and preserve it for the time being, if only as a gage for the money I claim.'

The registrar asked about Emma's expert. 'Will you be calling someone to prove what is wrong with your washing machine? If so, do you want him to be present when the defendant's expert is making his inspection? People sometimes feel happier if their own man is there on these occasions, you know. But it is up to you, Mrs. Seaton.'

'Well, sir,' said Emma 'I have in mind to bring as a witness just the man from the manufacturer who was supposed to have serviced the machine, and put the faults right when it went wrong. That in my view is the best evidence I can get about the matter. But of course he won't be willing to come and represent me, so to speak, at the proposed inspection of the machine, so that the question does not arise. By the way, I don't know if this is the right time to ask about this, but I shall need a witness summons to get that witness to come to court. Do I have to ask for that now?'

'No, you don't have to ask me for that,' said the registrar. 'In fact, you are entitled to come to the court office and obtain a witness summons any time you like, you don't have to apply to me personally for it. You can do it as soon as the date of the trial has been fixed. I will order that each side is confined to calling one expert engineering or mechanical witness.' The registrar made a note in his file to this effect, and Emma and Mr. Coales likewise made a note of it.

—special damage
'Now, let us look at the items of special damage,' said the registrar. 'Assuming that the claim is well founded, these seem on the whole reasonable. There's expenditure at the launderette, travelling expenses, and so forth. Obviously, Mrs. Seaton will have to prove by her own sworn testimony that she incurred these items. But we don't want to have to trouble her

to call witnesses about these comparitively trifling items. Surely, you can agree them, can't you, Mr. Coales, subject always to the question of liability?'

'I dare say we could,' said Mr. Coales. 'In fact, sir, on the assumption that we are found liable—which, of course, we deny—I think I can say that we can agree the items of special damage. That does not include, of course, the return of the purchase price.'

'Shall I record, therefore, that the items of special damage under paragraph 14 (2) of the particulars of claim are agreed, subject to liability?' And the registrar spoke as he was writing down a note about it. 'Good. Now we are getting somewhere.'

The registrar had succeeded in getting Watsons, through their solicitors, to accept the fact that, if the washing machine had gone wrong and if they were liable for it, Emma had reasonably incurred the out-of-pocket expenses she had claimed, and in the amounts she had specified in her particulars of claim. She would no longer have to prove this. The manageress from the launderette would not, after all, have to be dragged to court to prove what it had cost to wash a load of clothes.

—discovery

The registrar resumed his review of the case. 'That brings us to discovery, I suppose. Mrs. Seaton, I do not know how much you know of court procedure. But let me explain briefly what I am talking about. You are entitled to have access to all the documents which the defendants have in their possession or power, relating to this case. They have to disclose to you what documents they have, you are entitled to see them, and normally you can expect to be provided with a copy of any document you do not already have. In the same way, you have to reveal to them your documents. And you must not hide or destroy any of your documents, even a document which helps their case, but hinders yours. Do you understand? I would like you now to give some thought to this question, so far as it applies to this case. Now I expect you have some documents, don't you, Mrs. Seaton?'

'Well a few, sir. Not many, though,' said Emma. 'I have, as a matter of fact, already discussed discovery with Mr. Coales here, and we are more or less agreed, subject to your directions, of course, that there should be discovery. I am quite anxious to see some of Watsons records regarding this particular washing machine.'

The registrar turned to Mr. Coales and asked: 'You are agreed about discovery, then?'

'Yes, sir,' replied Mr. Coales. 'Lists would be appropriate, with inspection and copies in the usual way.'

'Well, then,' said the registrar. 'I will order discovery on lists within ten days. Could you prepare a list of your documents within ten days, both of you?' Both agreed that ten days would be fine.

This meant that each side would present to the other, within ten days, a list of their own documents, but without going to the further formality of swearing (on a sworn statement called an affidavit) that the list provided was complete. In other words, they agreed that they would trust each other to disclose on a list (without requiring that it should be sworn) what documents each possessed.

'All right', continued the registrar, 'and I will say inspection within seven days after that. I take it that you will both be able to agree a bundle of documents for the trial? You will be able to assist Mrs. Seaton in the preparation of a bundle, won't you, Mr. Coales?'

'Yes, sir, we will do what we can.' After each side has inspected the other side's documents, it is usual— where there are quite a lot of documents to be put before the court—to prepare several sets of bundles (correspondence in one, for instance, bills in another) combining documents from both sides into logical order.

—date of trial
To prevent any delaying on either side, and to produce a timetable of procedure, the registrar had imposed time limits on each side for producing lists of their own documents, and for inspecting the other side's documents. Having made a note of what had been decided regarding discovery, the registrar looked up and said: 'Anything else?'

'No, sir,' said Mr. Coales and Emma.

'Well, in that case, there is just the matter of fixing a date for the hearing of the case, if possible, and settling the details. Now, this will be a case for the judge to try, as the amount claimed is over £100. Let us have a look at the court diary, to see if we can fix a day here and now. It depends on how long this case will take to try. How many witnesses will there be on your side, Mrs. Seaton?'

'Well, it isn't finally settled yet, sir,' she replied 'but I imagine there will be myself, my husband, and the mechanic from the manufacturers. There may be one more, but I doubt it. That's just three, then.'

'And how about the defence?' the registrar asked of Mr. Coales.

'Only two witnesses, maybe three, sir,' said Mr. Coales.

'In that case,' said the registrar 'how long do you think? Could the case be over in half a day?' By this he meant would the case be finished in two and a half hours, since courts normally sit from 10.30 am to 1.0 pm, and 2 pm to 4.30 pm. He was only asking Emma out of politeness, as he knew she really had no idea.

'I am afraid I could not even begin to guess, sir. I have no experience of this sort of thing.'

'Well, we'll allow half a day. In which case, I think we could say the first open day in April, that means the first available day. We may be able to slip it in for the fourth of April.' The registrar turned to his clerk for confirmation about this, then said: 'The exact date will be notified to you in a few days.'

'We shall have counsel, of course,' said Leslie Coales. 'I do not know who it will be yet.'

Emma was not surprised to learn that Watsons intended to have counsel, that is a barrister, to fight their case for them. They could have had a solicitor——a partner in the firm of Dodds & Son, for instance——if they liked. There are many solicitors who are extremely experienced at county court work, and who would do the job just as well as, and in some instances better than, the average barrister. But those who can afford it generally prefer counsel to represent them.

'Well, that is all then,' said the registrar, 'thank you very much.' Emma and Mr. Coales thanked the registrar, got up and walked out of the court room. Once they were outside, they discussed how they were going to organise things between them from then on.

'With the hearing six weeks away, we are going to have to get a move on,' said Mr. Coales. 'By the time we have coped with discovery and all that, we are not going to have much time. I shall have to do a brief to counsel, and I suppose arrange about inspecting the washing machine. I hope we can fit it all in.'

'I'm all right myself for time, I think,' said Emma. 'But by all means let's get down to discovery immediately. What have we got to do?'

'Well,' said Mr. Coales, 'we have ten days officially to get our lists of documents prepared but there is no reason why we shouldn't try to do it a bit before then, is there? Can you get your list to me by this time next week? If so, I will try to do the same, and then we could arrange inspection by the end of next week, or anyway early in the week after.'

This was agreed. Emma would come to the office of Dodds & Son in Charter Street with her documents so that they could look at her documents while she looked at Watsons', all at the same meeting.

'See you, then,' said Mr. Coales and he politely bade her farewell.

Three days later Emma received the official order giving details of what had been decided at the pretrial review. This is what it said:

IN THE MINFORD COUNTY COURT

No. of plaint 73/00534

Between

Emma Caroline Seaton (married woman)   *Plaintiff*

and

Watsons Stores (Minford) Limited   *Defendant*

UPON HEARING the plaintiff in person and the solicitors for the Defendants
IT IS ORDERED that

1. The Plaintiff do within 10 days file in the Court Office a list of documents and deliver a copy to the Defendant.

2. The Defendant do within 10 days file in the Court Office a list of documents and deliver a copy to the Plaintiff.

3. There be inspection of documents within 7 days of the service of the lists.

4. A report by engineers be agreed if possible, and that, if not, the expert evidence be limited to one witness for each party.

5, The items of special damage totalling £12.40 set out in paragraph 14(2) of the particulars of claim are agreed between the parties subject to liability.

6. TRIAL. Estimated length: half a day.

7. The costs of the pre-trial review shall be costs in the cause.

AND IT IS ORDERED that the trial of the action shall be fixed for 4th April 1973 at 10.30 o'clock at the Court House, Minford County Court, Morris Street, Minford, Surrey.

Dated this 20th day of February 1973

H. L. Punton

Registrar

Paragraph 7 meant that whichever side won could count the expenses of attending the pre-trial review as legitimate expenses to recover from the loser.

witness summons

Now that she knew the date of the hearing, Emma could go to the court office to obtain a witness summons for procuring the attendance of the mechanic from Toltons.

It turned out to be a simple matter. 'I wish to issue a witness summons, please,' she said, showing her plaint note, which always had to be produced for any sort of application at the court office. The clerk brought out a form, called a request (formerly praecipe). It was simple to fill in. She had to write the name of her case in full, with the plaint number, and then state the name, address and occupation, as fully as she knew them, of the witness she required. Then she had to state whether she wanted the witness to bring any documents to court. If not, the rest of the form would not apply, and could simply be crossed out. This would mean that, when the witness summons was served, the witness would be required to bring nothing but himself to court for the hearing, merely to testify. But Emma needed Mr. Richardson. from the manufacturer of the washing machine, to bring the records they had about the machine, its servicing and so forth. This was most important. Without the documents, it was quite likely that Mr. Richardson would not be able to remember any of the significant details of the affair.

So Emma specified on the form: 'all documents

(e.g. records, service sheets, copy invoices, repair dockets, stock records) relating to a Washfaster Washing Machine sold to Mrs. Emma Seaton of 14 Twintree Avenue, Minford, Surrey, by Watsons Stores (Minford) Ltd in May 1972, together with all correspondence, notes, phone call records, and other documents in the possession of Toltons Domestic Appliances Limited relating to that machine'. The object was to define the list of documents as widely as possible. Emma did not really know just what documents there were. Her intention, therefore, was to request explicitly a number of the most likely ones. It was hardly conceivable that Toltons did not have stock records for instance, otherwise they would have no means of checking what went in and out of their premises; and some records about servicing given to appliances must be indispensable. So she picked out the most likely ones, then added, in effect, 'and any others you may have of a similar kind' for good measure. It is not essential to use the precise description as used in the organisation, provided that the general meaning is clear.

There might be a difficulty on the question of whether Mr. Richardson was the right man to produce all these documents. He probably had access to some of them—the servicing records, for instance, since he was himself part of the servicing department. But it might well be argued by Toltons that he had nothing to do with the stock records, or the invoices. They would probably be in the possession of the warehouse foreman, or the sales department. Mr. Richardson was nevertheless required to do what he could to produce them. If there were any he could not produce, then he would have to come along on the day to the court and say so. If the worst came to the worst, he could be asked (while standing in the witness box) who is the right man to produce any of the documents he cannot himself bring. Having identified the right man, another witness summons could be issued there and then, and the right man could be made to produce the documents, and the trial adjourned till he did so.

People are often not clear about the role of witnesses and documents in relation to court cases. They somehow feel it is wrong to trouble strangers or friends to have to come to court. And to ask someone to turn up and bring some private papers for a court to see may be thought little short of an impertinence. But if justice depends on it, the law says that people simply must reveal their documents, must come to court and explain what they saw or heard or did. It is on these grounds that a party to a court case can obtain, just for the asking, a witness summons, and require a witness to produce any documents relevant to the matters in dispute in the case.

The form asked by whom the witness summons was to be served. Emma thought for a moment and then asked the clerk 'What difference does it make?'

'Well the witness summons costs you 10p if you serve it yourself, and 85p if we do it,' said the clerk. For the sake of 75p Emma would have been happy for the court to do it, to save her the trouble. But it occurred to her, after reflecting, that it would be no bad thing for her to serve the witness summons herself. It would give her a chance to see Mr. Richardson personally and, with a bit of luck, to talk to him about the things he might be going to say in court about her washing machine. Even partially hostile witnesses are often willing, when it comes to it, to give a statement (or proof of evidence, as it is sometimes called), when they are actually confronted with the person who insists on their coming to court. It is more difficult to get any statement if the witness summons is served by the court bailiff. What is more, with a bit of luck, Toltons might let Emma see the documents she wished them to produce, if she gave them a bit of notice. So this is what she decided to do: serve the witness summons herself, having given Mr. Richardson himself, and Toltons in general, fair notice in advance that she was coming to serve the summons on a particular day at a particular time.

'I will serve the witness summons myself, please,' Emma told the clerk at the court. She produced 10p from her handbag, and made a note of this expense on the memorandum regarding her costs and expenses of the court case, which she was keeping. The clerk took a bit of time to make out the actual witness summons, in duplicate. He gave her the two copies, both bearing the court seal which made them official. 'You know,' he told her 'that you have to serve a witness summons personally. That is, you have to give it to the actual man himself. You cannot send it through the post. Another thing—you will have to come back here after serving it, within three days, to swear an affidavit of service.' He handed her a blank form of affidavit for this. 'And you know about conduct money, do you?' he asked. 'Whenever you serve a witness summons, you have to give the witness enough money to get from his home, or his office or wherever he would normally be, to the court and back. You have to pay his fares in advance, in fact, otherwise he could say he could not afford to get here under his own steam. Even if he lives next-door to the court, you have to pay him 5p. In addition, you have to give him something to compensate him for his loss of time. It's only something on account, as you might say. He will get more, as a rule, once he has given his evidence. There's a sliding scale: £4 for a boss, £1·50 for everybody else, more or less. They get the rest once they have given their evidence. Anyway, you will want to make sure you offer this chap his conduct money when you serve the summons.'

Emma examined the two copies of the witness summons carefully. She made sure that the names, addresses and particulars (especially those regarding the sought-for documents) were correct. The clerk further explained: 'You'll see that there is a place on the back to fill in the details of when and where the summons was served. Ignore it—it is only needed if the bailiff serves it. In your case, you will have to swear the affidavit of service instead.'

forms

Emma had planned a shopping expedition to London at about this time, and she took the opportunity of visiting the Oyez shop run by The Solicitors Law Stationery Society Ltd, in Hanover Street, near Oxford Circus, to buy some legal forms. There are Oyez shops or sales offices in several other places in London, and in various parts of the country. You do not have to be a solicitor to buy county court forms; and you can write for them to Oyez Publishing Ltd, 237 Long Lane, London SE1 (tel. 01-407 8055), if this is more convenient. Emma bought the following forms:

Form C.C. 83A: List of documents (4 copies)

Form C.C. 119: Notice to admit documents (2 copies)

Form C.C. 120: Notice to produce documents at hearing (2 copies)

Those forms cost her altogether 57p; if she had ordered them by post or phone, rather than in person and asked for the forms to be sent to her, there would have been 44p to add for post, packing and handling charge.

At this stage, the form she really needed was the list of documents, form C.C. 83A, but she thought she might as well get the others while she was there.

There is no need to use the printed forms produced by law stationers for any of the documents required in connection with a county court case. But when it comes to coping with discovery of documents, using a printed form is helpful. For one thing, there is a prescribed and rather wordy formula used for the list of documents, and she was more or less bound to adopt the standard wording of this.

Emma bought four copies of form C.C. 83A although she might have managed with three. She would use one copy for drafting the document, the rough version, which would probably end up with lots of crossings-out, and so not be suitable for use as an original. The second copy was for the original, the posh copy, which she would send to the court when it was ready. The third copy was for Dodds & Son. And the fourth was a clean copy for her to keep.

list of documents
The registrar had made an order, in the course of the pre-trail review, that each side was to reveal to the other what documents he or she had. He said that this was to bc donc on 'lists'. This meant that each side would prepare a formal list, stating what documents there were. There is a rule that each side must do this using the appropriate wording laid down in the County Court Rules, although in practice it is often done informally in an exchange of letters. Emma was using form C.C. 83A—list of documents—for this purpose. It was a printed form with blanks to fill in. The important parts, for anyone reading the document, were the two schedules to the form. The first schedule contained a space where Emma would list the documents which she actually had in her possession. In part I of the first schedule she would list all the documents she had to disclose. Part II of the first schedule set out the documents which Emma had in her possession, but which she claimed she was not bound to disclose. These are the so-called privileged documents—those that are protected from disclosure. Only a few kinds of documents are immune in this way. They include letters to and from one's own solicitor (if one has a solicitor), counsel's opinions, draft documents, and notes made about one's own case. Emma did not want Dodds & Son to see her own

private jottings, revealing her notes about the case. To prevent her having to show these notes to Dodds & Son she would have to claim privilege, by referring to them in part II of the first schedule to the list of documents. This she did.

The second schedule to the form called 'List of Documents' was the place for listing any documents which Emma once had in her possession, and which were no longer in her possession. In a simple case, like Emma's, this consisted of nothing but the original letters she had written to other people.

Emma arranged all the documents she had to disclose carefully into two piles—those she had to reveal and those for which she was claiming privilege. Then she completed form C.C.83A. This is how it read:

IN THE MINFORD COUNTY COURT
C.C. 83A   Plaint No.*73/00534*
Between
Emma Caroline Seaton   Plaintiff
        and
Watsons' Stores (Minford) Limited   Defendant

I, *Emma Caroline Seaton*
of *14 Twintree Avenue, Minford, Surrey*
the above-named *plaintiff*   say as follows:

1. I have in my possession or power the Documents relating to the matters in question in these proceedings set forth in the first and second parts of the First Schedule hereto.

2. I object to produce the said Documents set forth in the second part of the said First Schedule hereto.

3. That the grounds on which I so object to produce the said Documents are that such Documents are as appears

from their nature privileged for the following reasons namely: *They are notes and draft documents prepared by me in connection with this case for the purpose of bringing this case, and preparing the case for the trial.*

4. I have had, but have not now, in my possession or power the Documents relating to the matters in question in these proceedings set forth in the Second Schedule hereto.

5. The last-mentioned Documents were last in my possession or power on the day *when each letter as listed was posted* and they are now in the hands of *the recipients.*

6. That the said Documents left my possession or power under the following circumstances:
I sent the letters concerned to the people to whom they were addressed, and they are now in the hands of *those people.*

7. According to the best of my knowledge, information and belief, I have not now, and never had in my possession, custody or power, or in the possession, custody or power of my Solicitor, or in the possession, custody or power of any other person on my behalf, any deed, account, book of account, voucher, receipt, letter, memorandum, paper, or writing, or any copy of or extract from any such Document, or any other Document whatsoever, relating to the matters in question in these proceedings, or any of them, or wherein any entry has been made relative to such matters, or any of them, other than and except the Documents set forth in the said First and Second Schedules hereto.

THE FIRST SCHEDULE—PART I

Description of Document	Date
Bill from Watsons Stores (Minford) Ltd for Washfaster Washing Machine: Ref MX/24759/DB	*1 May 1972*
Guarantee for the machine from Toltons Domestic Appliances Ltd.	*undated*
Instructions for use for the machine	*undated*
Service vouchers from Toltons Domestic Appliances Ltd.	*5 June 1972* *11 Aug 1972* *3 Nov 1972*
Copies of letters from myself to Watsons	*11 Dec 1972* *17 Dec 1972*
Letters from Watsons to myself	*14 Dec 1972* *21 Dec 1972*
Letters from Dodds & Son to myself	*19 Jan 1973* *12 Feb 1973*
Copies of letters from myself to Dodds & Son	*24 Jan 1973* *4 Feb 1973*
Copies of letters from myself to Toltons Domestic Appliances Ltd	*11 Dec 1972* *24 Jan 1973*
Letter from Toltons to myself	*31 Jan 1973*

THE FIRST SCHEDULE—PART II

Description of Document	Date
Various notes and draft documents prepared by me for the purpose of bringing this case, and preparing this case for trial	*Various*

THE SECOND SCHEDULE

Letters from me to Watsons, their solicitors (Dodds & Son) and to Toltons, the copies of which are detailed as items in the first part of the first schedule above	*On the dates of such copy letters as shown above*
Paid cheque for £84.50 myself to Watsons Ltd (thrown away)	*1 May 1972*

Dated the *25th* day of *February 1973*

(Signed) *Emma C. Seaton*

This was a formidable way of saying something which was in fact comparatively simple. In effect, all the list of documents said was this:

'These are the documents I have to disclose. Those listed in the first schedule, part 1 are all the ones I have in my possession now, which I agree I must disclose. Those in the first schedule, part 2 I will not disclose, because I am not bound to do so—they are privileged. Those in the second schedule are the documents the originals of which I no longer have in my possession.'

Emma sent the list of documents to the court, with a note 'from Mrs. Emma Seaton, plaintiff's list of documents: Seaton v Watsons Stores (Minford) Ltd Plaint No 73/00534'.

She now wrote to Dodds & Son:

> 14 Twintree Avenue,
> Minford, Surrey.
> 25 February 1973

Dear Sirs,

> *Myself v Watsons*

I now enclose my list of documents. Please acknowledge receipt and let me have your client's list of documents as soon as possible. We can then arrange an appointment for each side to inspect the other's documents.

In the meantime, may I remind you that at the pre-trial review the question was raised of your client's expert inspecting the washing machine at my house. No doubt you will phone for an appointment for this to be done shortly.

> Yours faithfully,
> Emma Seaton

Messrs. Dodds & Son.

On the same day Emma wrote to Mr. Richardson, the mechanic from Toltons:

> 14 Twintree Avenue,
> Minford, Surrey.
> 25 February 1973

Dear Sir,

> *Myself v Watsons Stores (Minford) Ltd*

As you may know from previous correspondence, I am now suing Watsons Stores about the defective Washfaster washing machine they sold me, which was manufactured by your company and serviced by you.

In my letter of 24 January to your company I explained that it would be necessary for me to ask you to give evidence at the trial of my case. Your Mr. Bugden in his letter to me of 31 January was unable to undertake that you would come to the Minford County Court voluntarily to give evidence for me. I have, therefore, obtained a witness summons bearing your name which will, when served, require you to attend court.

I am writing to tell you that the hearing of my case has been fixed for 4 April 1973 at Minford County Court, Morris Street, Minford, and I shall be obliged if you will kindly arrange to keep that day free for this purpose. Please come to the court at 10.30 am and meet me in the concourse of the court building, at that time on that day.

I should now like to arrange an appointment for me to serve you with the witness summons. Please phone me within the next 7 days to make an appointment for this purpose. I have in mind that I should visit the depot of your company one morning. I would like at the same time to ask you to provide me with a statement regarding the evidence you can give.

Finally, the witness summons will require you to produce at the hearing the following documents in the possession of your employers, Toltons Domestic Appliances Ltd: 'all documents (e.g. records, service sheets, copy invoices, repair dockets, stock records) relating to a Washfaster Washing Machine sold to Mrs. Emma Seaton of 14 Twintree Avenue, Minford, Surrey, by Watsons Stores (Minford) Ltd in May 1972, together with all correspondence, notes, phone call records, and other documents in the possession of Toltons Domestic Appliances Ltd relating to that machine'.

I shall be grateful if you will arrange to have ready those documents for my inspection when I call on you to serve the witness summons. It would be a convenience to myself, and to the court at the trial, if you and your company were able to provide me with copies of these documents when I call on you, so that there may be an opportunity of studying them before the trial.

I look forward to hearing from you.

Yours faithfully,
Emma Seaton

Mr. David Richardson,
Toltons Domestic Appliances Ltd.

It is not always wise to write and warn a person that you have a witness summons you wish to serve on him. In some cases, the effect is to make him do his best to avoid you. If you suspect that this is likely to happen, the better course is to turn up on his doorstep without warning, and just give him the witness summons. If he will not take hold of it, put it down in his presence and tell him what it is. But when you are dealing with an established company, an official organisation (such as the police or a government or local authority department) or a moderately friendly person, it is often better to make the arrangements by correspondence, and to keep them informed about what is happening, and what your requirements will be. They usually accept that you can compel them to attend court, and that it makes it easier for them, as well as for you, if the whole business is handled in a pleasant and co-operative way. Some organisations— the police, for example—make it a rule not to let their employees attend court voluntarily, always insisting that a witness summons be procured and served. In this way they cannot be accused of taking sides in the dispute, as they can justly claim that they had no option but to attend. It by no means follows just because a person refuses to give evidence for you unless served with a witness summons, that he will necessarily be obstructive or unco-operative.

It is one thing to require a witness to come to court: he has no option. It is quite another to get him to tell you before he comes to court what he will be going to say. And it may be even more difficult to get him to show you in advance any of the documents he is required to produce in court. But in practice, a witness, once served with a witness summons, may well let you take a statement from him. He may be more cagey about handing over documents, but he may provide copies for you. Once he realises that he has to produce the documents at the trial, he may let you study them in advance.

It is wise to be tactful in writing to a potential witness. Coax him towards co-operation, rather than use sledgehammer tactics. Emma's letter to Mr. Richardson, in fact, made it rather hard for him to refuse what she asked. It also spelled out quite clearly what she wanted, giving him time to think it over, take advice, and assemble the required documents.

the other side's list of documents
Within a few days, Emma heard from Dodds & Son with their list of documents. As with hers, it was typed on form C.C. 83A, and the important part was found in the documents listed in the first and second schedules, although not much was revealed to Emma by the list. Only when she came to inspect the documents themselves would she find out whether her case was helped by having access to Watsons' documents. But, looking at their list, she was able to get some idea of what she might find. On the whole, it was quite encouraging. The first schedule, part I, was where they listed the documents they had in their possession, and which they were required to disclose to Emma. These were the documents listed:

THE FIRST SCHEDULE—PART I

Description of Document	Date
Stock records regarding Washfaster DB 8732/67G, ref. 24759:	
Delivery note from supplier	6 April 1971
Goods inwards note	6 April 1971
Warehouse stock records card	various
Delivery—goods outward—note	5 May 1972
Invoice from Supplier	5 April 1971
Copy invoice to customer	1 May 1972
Customers order	
order form	1 May 1972
order docket	5 May 1972
Account book entries	
bought ledger	April/May 1971
sales ledger	May 1972
Correspondence:	
Letters from Mrs. E. Seaton	11 Dec 1972
	17 Dec 1972
copy letters to—ditto	14,21 Dec 1972
copy letter to Toltons Domestic Appliances Ltd	14 Dec 1972
letter from—ditto	20 Dec 1972
Internal memos	
Memo from Managing Director to Sales Manager	15 Dec 1972
Memo from Sales Manager to Managing Director	15 Dec 1972

Emma was able to glean from this list that the washing machine had apparently been bought by

Watsons in April 1971, thirteen months before they
sold it to her, in May 1972. Why had it been in stock
so long? This could only be a matter for speculation
at this stage. Then there was the exchange between
the managing director and the sales manager. She
could not wait to see what it contained.

She considered whether there was any indication
that they may have left out any documents she would
be entitled to see. Did it all make sense? Could it be
that something was being supressed?

The first schedule, part II, of the list set out the
documents which Watsons objected to producing, on
the grounds that they were privileged. This included
the notes and memoranda which Dodds & Son had
made in preparing the case, and which had come into
existence since the case had begun. These were on a
par with the private notes for which Emma had
claimed privilege in her list of documents a few days
before. Then they claimed privilege for the correspondence between Watsons and Dodds & Son. These
were privileged because they were communications
between a solicitor and his client. The same applied
to the counsel's written opinion which they had
obtained, no doubt from the barrister whose name
had appeared at the foot of the defence, Mr. Keith
Sanders. Legal advice from a lawyer to a client—
whether the lawyer is a solicitor or a barrister, and
whether it is oral or in writing—is protected from
disclosure to the court or to the other side in legal
proceedings. In the same way, a witness would not be
obliged to answer, if, in giving evidence in court, he
were asked: 'And what advice did your solicitor or

your counsel then give you about what to do next?' Such matters are protected from disclosure, even in court, because of the importance the law attaches to complete candour in discussions between lawyer and client. Only if the client agrees to forgo the privilege can the lawyer be required to give evidence about what transpired between them.

The rest of the list of documents—the second schedule, in fact—merely listed the documents which Watsons no longer had in their possession, but once did. They were the original letters that Watsons had written to Emma herself and to Toltons. The correspondence between Watsons and Toltons would also be interesting for her to see, and Emma made a note to read those letters carefully.

Emma now knew what to look for when inspection of documents took place. This was one of the things referred to in the letter she had received from Dodds & Son sending the list of documents. This is what the letter said:

1 Charter Street,
Minford, Surrey.
27th February 1973

Dear Madam,

Watsons ats Seaton

Thank you for your letter of 25th February enclosing your list of documents. In reply we now enclose our client's list of documents, safe receipt of which please acknowledge.

You will recall that at the pre-trial review you kindly agreed that inspection of documents should take place at our office, and we suggest that this be on Tuesday next, 6th of March, at 3 pm. Please telephone us if this is not convenient, when another appointment can be arranged.

We confirm that you should bring with you for our inspection all the documents you have disclosed in your list, and we will in turn produce for your inspection the documents shown in the enclosed list. We have photocopying facilities here, and as you do not have very many documents you may find it convenient to have your documents copied while you are visiting our offices.

We presume that you will require copies of our client's documents, as shown in the First Schedule, part I to the enclosed list of documents. If so, we will provide you with copies of these when you call here. It is the practice for each side to pay for copy documents supplied in this way, and we shall ask you for the sum of £1.20 per set to cover the cost of copying the said documents. Please confirm that these arrangements are agreed by you.

Regarding the proposed inspection of the washing machine at your premises, we have retained on behalf of our clients the services of a consulting engineer, Mr. R. J. Ardern AMIMechE, and have asked him to telephone you direct to make an appointment to inspect the same at your premises at a mutually convenient time. We do not intend to be present, and shall be glad if you will deal direct with him and provide the requisite facilities for inspection. If there is any difficulty in this regard, no doubt you will let us know.

> *Yours faithfully,*
> *Dodds & Son*

Mrs. Emma Seaton.

The arrangements Dodds & Son proposed for inspecting documents seemed convenient. Emma phoned Dodds & Son agreeing the time they suggested for inspection of documents. Formally, the object of inspection is for each side to inspect the other side's documents. In practice, copies of documents the other side requires are usually mutually provided as well. In the old days, documents were laboriously copied by hand. There is no obligation on either side to supply copies of documents free. Any copies supplied are normally paid for, charging the estimated cost (in time and expenditure) of producing them. Each side then pays for what it gets, and these expenses form part of the court costs which can be recovered by the winner from the loser when the case is over.

inspection of the washing machine

The arrangements about the inspection of the washing machine by the expert engineer on behalf of Watsons were acceptable from Emma's point of view. Mr. Ardern, in fact, phoned the day after the letter came and made an appointment to come and see the machine the day after that. He turned out to be a bluff, cheerful man. He carefully took the machine to pieces and examined the inside. He made a number of notes. Emma had no compunction in standing over and watching him as he went through the routine of examining the machine. She could not afford to trust anyone in this situation and it seemed right that she should be present throughout, to make sure that he did not slip a new part in here, or craftily change a bolt there, and so distort the evidence in some way. Emma felt confident that Mr. Ardern would not be doing such a thing. But people are not always what they seem.

Not surprisingly, he gave nothing away about what he was finding inside the machine, and Emma did not attempt to pump him for information about this. But she did have a pencil and notebook to hand throughout his examination, and made notes of what happened: the time he arrived, what he dismantled in the machine (so far as she could follow it), what he examined, how long he took about each stage of his examination, and what he did when he reassembled the machine. Both he and she realised that she might have to cross-examine him about his findings, at the trial. It was well while therefore, for Emma to make careful notes of all that happened, as it happened. A reliable record, even in rough note form, is better than reliance on memory. This is why a policeman always carries a notebook.

When Mr. Ardern had finished, he tidied up, and left. Emma read through her notes immediately, to make sure that they made sense, amended a word or two, and topped and tailed her notes: 'Notes of inspection of Washfaster washing machine by Mr. R. J. Ardern on behalf of Watsons: 2 March 1973, at 3.20 pm in the presence of Mrs. E. C. Seaton'. At the bottom she wrote: 'I have read and corrected these notes and they accurately set out the main events of the inspection. Signed Emma Seaton 2 March 1973, 5.15 pm.'

Notes such as these do not constitute a piece of evidence in themselves, in the way that a letter does, but they can be used by a witness to look at while giving evidence to refresh his or her memory.

inspection of documents

On 6 March, the day fixed for the inspection of the

documents, Emma separated out the documents she had to show to Dodds & Son from all the rest, and made sure that the documents she was required to disclose were seperately clipped together. At Dodds & Son's offices she found she was with the same young man she had met at the pre-trial review, Mr. Leslie Coales. He greeted her and they immediately got down to the business in hand.

'Let's deal with your documents, first, shall we?' he asked. 'If we are going to copy them here and now, it will take a bit of time, and you can be looking at ours, while yours are being copied. Is that all right?' Emma agreed.

She handed over the documents one by one. Mr. Coales glanced at each one as Emma handed it to him to check that it was described in the list. When she reached the correspondence between Emma and Watsons, Mr. Coales said: 'I don't need to see these letters, as I already have them. They are mutual, as we say; from you to me or my people, and vice versa.' And with that, he handed the letters to and from Watsons and Dodds & Son back to Emma. He collected together the documents which were new to him, and said: 'Right, I will get someone to copy these now. How many copies of each one do you think we need?'

'What usually happens?' asked Emma.

'Well it depends,' said Mr. Coales. 'Let's work it out. We shall need one copy for ourselves, one for counsel. Then there is one for the judge, and one for you. That's four. Do you think that's enough? We don't need a spare, do we?'

Emma agreed that a spare set of copies was not needed. There were always the originals that someone could look at, after all. They agreed that four copies of each document should be made, one set of which would come back to Emma together with the originals.

A secretary appeared and took away Emma's original documents for copying. While that was being done, Mr. Coales handed to her the originals of the documents Watsons had disclosed in their list of documents, together with a set of copies of them, already prepared. No correspondence after the summons had been issued was included, as this was most unlikely to be needed at the trial.

Emma took from her file Watsons' list of documents, and checked off the originals, and the set of copies, one by one, against the list, just as Mr. Coales had done in the case of her documents a few minutes previously. She would have a chance to study the papers when she got home. At this stage she concentrated on comparing the originals with the copies. No matter how good the method of photocopying, there may be something about an original document which is not quite reproduced in a photocopy. Sometimes the bottom line or two of a page gets cut off in the copying, or the copy is not very clear. It pays to give the original some scrutiny, therefore. It is useful to look at an original (the back as well as the front) to see whether any pencil notes, or other additions or alterations appear there.

Emma made a few notes (on a seperate piece of paper, not on the copies) about some of the documents, where the copy did not quite convey the full flavour of the original. This was, in practice, her last chance to study with care the original documents produced by the other side. When it came to the hearing, and she was cross-examining Watsons' witnesses about these documents, she would have in her hand the copies, while the witness would have the original.

The last documents they disclosed were the internal memos passing between Watsons' managing director and their sales manager. Emma had hopes of these, but they turned out to be rather a disappointment. The memo from the managing director just said: 'Jim, what's all this about some woman threatening to sue us about a washing machine or something? What is it all about'. The reply was: 'We have put her on to the makers (Toltons), who guarantee the thing, and told her that it is nothing to do with us. One of these professional complainers, I dare say. Toltons will sort it out. Nothing to worry about.'

Before long the girl returned with Emma's documents and four sets of copies of them. Emma checked that she was getting all her originals back again, and put them into the right order. She also checked the set of copies she had obtained, to see that it was complete.

'There's just one more thing,' said Mr. Coales. 'We ought to agree just how we are going to arrange all these documents, so that we can easily find what we want, when it comes to the trial. The usual thing is to arrange them into bundles. But I am not sure that there is enough in this case to merit it.' He examined all the documents. 'I don't know, though. How about making them into three bundles,' he said. 'Bundle A can be the correspondence between the two of us—your letters to our clients and to us, arranged in date order. The mutual documents, you remember. That's bundle A'. He sorted them out to make them into a separate pile. 'Then bundle B can be your own documents, apart from these mutual letters; starting with this invoice for your machine and including your correspondence with Toltons, in date order again. And bundle C can be my clients', that is Watsons', documents, apart from those in bundle A.'

They arranged the documents into these three bundles. They each compiled, using copies, a specimen of the agreed bundles, made sure that each was complete and identical, and then went through each bundle numbering the documents. In this way, each document had a number from which it could be identified, for instance A5, and B2 and C3 and so on.

'Just one more thing,' said Mr. Coales. 'Would you mind now paying for the cost of copying documents. First there is twice £1.20, for my client's documents (one set for you, and one for the judge), and copies of your documents, two sets—for yourself and for the judge comes to twice 95p, that is £1.90.' Emma added it up and gave him £4.30. 'Thank you,' said Mr. Coales and gave her a receipt. 'See you at the trial.' That ended the interview, and Emma left the office.

That evening, Emma studied Watsons' documents with care. While she was about it, she decided to finish off the formalities regarding documents. Two new documents had to be prepared and sent to Dodds &

Son. One was called notice to produce and the other notice to admit. For each of them Emma used one of the printed forms she had obtained from the Oyez shop. Preparation of the documents involved little more than filling in the blanks in forms.

notice to produce

Emma used form C.C. 120, the full title of which is notice to produce documents at hearing. The purpose of this document is quite simple. It is a message to the other side to say: make sure you bring to the trial all the documents you have in your possession, and in particular those that you have disclosed in the process of discovery of documents.

It does not necessarily follow from the fact that one party has disclosed all his documents to his opponent that he will automatically produce them at the trial. 'I know you asked to see them,' he might, in theory, say, 'but you didn't say you wanted to rely on them at the trial. If you wanted them there, you should have told me.' To prevent him being able to say this, you send him notice to produce, telling him he must. If he does not, you are entitled to prove his documents by putting in your copies—one of the few cases where copies are allowed without the originals also being in court. To serve notice to produce is a formality, but quite an important one.

It is rather more important to send a notice to produce where there has not been discovery of documents. You can almost (not quite) assume, if a person discloses documents on discovery, that he will have the original documents in court for the trial. But where—as often happens in simple county court cases—there is no formal discovery, such an assumption is not justified.

Whether or not there has been discovery, in many cases a letter will do, saying: 'Please produce at the hearing all your documents relating to this case, especially ....' and then you specify any which you know he has, which you particularly want produced. Emma did it formally. This is how her notice to produce was worded:

In the Minford County Court

Plaint No. *73/00534*

Between
Mrs. Emma Caroline Seaton   Plaintiff
and
Watsons Stores (Minford) Limited   Defendant

Take Notice that you are hereby required to produce and show to the Court on the hearing of this *action* all books, papers, letters, copies of letters and other writings and documents in your custody, possession or power, containing any entry, memorandum or minute relating to the matters in question in this *action* and particularly *the documents specified in the first schedule part I of the defendant's list of documents in this case dated 27 February 1973.*

Dated the *6th* day of *March* 1973.
To the above-named   (Signed) *Emma Seaton*
defendant
and to   of *14 Twintree Avenue,*
Dodds & Son   *Minford Surrey*
their Solicitors   the above named *plaintiff*

If there had been no discovery of documents in Emma's case, she would have listed in the notice to produce all the documents she knew the defendant had, and which she wished to get her hands on. This was not necessary in her situation.

notice to admit

The other document she now prepared was called a notice to admit documents. For this she used form C.C.119. The purpose of this is to notify the other side that you will be relying on the documents listed in the notice to admit, that is the documents you will produce to the court. It arises in this way: documents are not assumed to be authentic and therefore have either to be admitted or to be proved in a court case. (There are a few exceptions, such as birth certificates.) For instance, you usually have to prove by proper evidence that the writer of a letter actually wrote it, posted it, or that the recipient received it. In some cases this is not too difficult—you simply call the writer or the recipient as a witness and they say on oath in court: 'This is the letter I wrote' or 'I received it'. But you may not want to, or not be able to call the writer or the recipient just to prove that one fact. It might be quite expensive and troublesome to do so. This is where the notice to admit comes in. The other side is asked to agree that each of the listed documents is authentic and not a forgery; furthermore to agree that it was duly sent or delivered in the way in which, on the face of it, one would assume it was. In other words, when you send a notice to admit documents you invite the other side to accept the gen-

uineness of your documents. If he does nothing, you
are saved the trouble and expense of producing at the
trial formal proof about the origin, text and transmis-
sion of each document listed.

In Emma's case, the notice to admit read:

Notice to admit documents.
IN THE MINFORD COUNTY COURT

Plaint No. *73/00534*

Between
Mrs. Emma Caroline Seaton   Plaintiff
    and
Watsons Stores (Minford) Limited   Defendant

Take Notice that *I, the plaintiff* in this action propose to
adduce in evidence the several document hereunder specified, and that the same may be inspected by the *defendant or their* Solicitors at *14 Twintree Avenue, Minford,
Surrey*
on *Friday*, the *9th* day of *March 1973*, between the hours
of *10 am* and *12.30 pm*; and the *defendant* is hereby
required within three days after receipt of this notice to
admit, saving all just exceptions to the admissibility of all
such documents as evidence in this action, that such of the
said documents as are specified to be originals were respectively written, signed or executed as they purport respectively to have been; that such as are specified as copies are
true copies; and that such documents as are stated to have
been served, sent or delivered, were so served, sent or
delivered respectively.

Dated this *6th* day of *March 1973*

(Signed) *Emma Seaton*
Plaintiff

To *Messrs Dodds & Son,*
1 Charter Street, Minford, Solicitors

ORIGINALS

Description of Document	Dates
The documents listed in the first schedule part I of the plaintiff's list of documents in this case, dated 25 February, 1973	*As shown in the plaintiff's list of documents*

(on reverse of page)

COPIES

Description of Document	Dates	Original or duplicate served, sent or delivered, when, how, and by whom
The documents listed in the second schedule of the plaintiff's list of documents in this case, dated 25 February 1973	*as shown in the plaintiff's list of documents*	*By post to the stated recipient on or about the day of its date*

C.C.119

Emma kept one copy of documents C.C.119 and C.C.120 as her copies, and prepared clean versions to send to Dodds & Son. She then wrote to Dodds & Son:

14 Twintree Avenue,
Minford, Surrey.
8 March 1973

Dear Sirs,

Myself v Watsons

I now enclose notice to produce and notice to admit. Please acknowledge receipt.

Yours faithfully,
Emma Seaton

Messrs. Dodds & Son.

In reply she received, as well as an acknowledgement of her letter, corresponding notices from Dodds & Son, requiring her to produce and admit Watsons' documents. So now each side had set its house in order on this score. As expected, neither side took the opportunity that was offered of a further inspection of the other side's documents. Neither side would be required to place before the court formal proof as to the making and sending of any of the documents. This was the last step in the preparation of the case for trial, so far as documents were concerned.

service of witness summons

Soon after the pre-trial review Emma had obtained a witness summons from the court, and had written to Mr. Richardson at Toltons, the company he worked for, asking for an appointment to come and serve it, and to discuss the evidence he would give. She had deliberately set a 7 day time limit for getting a reply to this letter, as she had suspected that it might well be ignored. Just as she was wondering whether she would have to drop in on Mr. Richardson without an appointment, she received a letter from solicitors acting for Toltons:

Kingsley & Wainright   184 Bedford Row,
Solicitors   London WC2
                                        8th March 1973

Dear Madam,

We are acting for Toltons Domestic Appliances Limited, and have received from them the letters you have written to them regarding the appliance manufactured by them, including your most recent letter dated 25th February in which you state that you have issued a witness summons in the Minford County Court for the attendance of their employee, Mr. David Richardson.

Our clients have no wish to become involved in this litigation, but as a witness summons has been issued, it would not be their purpose to obstruct the service thereof. We are instructed to suggest, therefore, that you may attend at the premises of our clients at 349 Godalming Road, Guildford on any day in the coming week at 9.30 am. You are asked to telephone direct before that time on any day to make an appointment.

Our clients are anxious not to be unhelpful to you, but in view of their obvious interest in the subject matter of these proceedings, they cannot assist you by providing a statement of the evidence Mr. Richardson can give. We are instructed that his evidence is not of any relevance to the matters in issue in this case. However, Mr. Richardson will be willing to discuss in general terms with you the course of events when he visited your premises on sundry occasions last year to attend to the washing machine manufactured by our clients. He will not, however, go beyond that and will not be willing to sign any statement. His supervisor Mr. A. H. Evans, will be present when you see Mr. Richardson, and you should ask for Mr. Evans when phoning for an appointment.

               Yours faithfully,
               Kingsley & Wainright.
To: Mrs. Emma C. Seaton.

Emma noticed that this letter made no reference to the important question of documents. She would have to wait to see what happened at the meeting with Mr. Evans and Mr. Richardson, before she knew what Toltons' attitude would be to showing their documents to her in advance of the trial of her case.

Emma wasted no time, and rang Mr. Evans at the Guildford number of Toltons as soon as she had read the letter from their solicitors. She made an appointment for the following monday.

She asked for Mr. Evans at reception, and was shown to his office. Mr. Evans was there with Mr. Richardson. After a formal exchange of greetings (warm on Emma's side, cool on the other), Emma got down to business.

'Firstly, I think that I should serve the witness summons on Mr. Richardson,' she said to Mr. Evans. She produced the summons she had obtained from the county court. 'I will hand it to you personally, if I may,' she said, turning to Mr. Richardson. She proffered the summons. Mr. Richardson backed away slightly, but she thrust it at him. Mr. Richardson looked towards his boss, who nodded at him, indicating that he should take it. This he did. 'I won't read it right through now. You can do that when I have gone, but the essence of it, you will see, is that you are required to attend at Minford County Court (the address is given there) on the fourth of April, at 10.30 am.'

'In order to make this witness summons legal,' she continued 'I have to give you what is called conduct money. That is, sufficient cash to enable you to get to and from the court on the day. Now, how will you be travelling?'

'Well, I may as well come in the firm's van, I suppose,' said Mr. Richardson. 'There's no public transport between here and Minford to speak of.'

'But I still have to give you enough cash to cover the bus fare, which in this case is 25p, plus 25p for coming back,' said Emma. 'In addition, I have to give you something on account of your time. This depends on the sort of job you have, and the rules provide that I should pay you £1.50 at this stage. You get some more afterwards. So I'm now handing to you £2 by way of conduct money.' She held out two pound notes. Mr. Richardson took them rather diffidently.

'I will just make a note that I have served the summons and paid you £2 for conduct money,' said Emma, implying (as was the case) that she did not require a receipt for the money, so long as she made a clear, dated note for herself that the summons had been served and the money paid.

'Now then,' said Emma 'if you read on, you will see that the witness summons refers to the documents that you are required to produce in the court. They represent, as you can see, just about every document that your company has in its possession which has any reference to my washing machine. That includes references to it when it was being serviced by you, as well as when it was being manufactured. I hope that is clear.' Both men looked vexed. It seemed to go right against the grain to them to have to reveal documents to strangers in this way. But both had obviously received advice from their superiors, no doubt originating from Toltons' solicitors, Kingsley an I Wainright.

Mr. Evans now took over. 'Yes, well this seems to me all very irregular, that you should be able to come in here and demand to see the company's private records. But I have my orders, and these are that you should be allowed to have a look at these records—I have them here.' He patted a file which lay on a desk before him. 'But my instructions are that you are not entitled to take any documents away with you, and that we should not provide any copies.'

'Thats all right by me,' said Emma. 'Just to get it quite straight, the legal position is that you are not required to show me any documents at this stage at all, but you are, of course, required to bring them to court, as stated in this witness summons which I have just served. I did ask to be provided with copies when I wrote to you, as you may remember, but you are quite within your rights in refusing me that. It will mean, however, that we shall have to spend a considerably longer period this morning while I go through the documents, and make notes of them. I should then like to ask some questions. I hope that will be all right?'

'Well, dealing with the last point first,' said Mr. Evans. 'I personally do not come into this, as you have not served anything on me. So don't expect me to give you any information. My colleague Mr. Richardson will give you general information only, those are his orders. I shall remain here to see that this is what happens. Though what they mean by general information I do not quite gather. Anyway, what is the next matter you require? These documents?'

Emma smiled at Mr. Evans. 'Yes, please. I think it would be much better if I saw the documents first and then talked to Mr. Richardson. Otherwise I shall only have to talk to him again when I have seen them, don't you think?'

'Very well, then,' said Mr. Evans, and with that he handed over to her the file in front of him, unopened. When she opened the file, she was reminded of when she first set eyes on Watsons' documents, not many days before. As then, at first, she found it hard to understand what the documents were all about, but gradually she made some sense of them. She ventured a question to Mr. Evans about one of them. 'I wonder, could you tell me what sort of record this is, please? It doesn't seem to have a title to it.' She picked up the document she had been looking at, and handed it back to Mr. Evans.

'That's a production slip, we call it. It is for recording...' His voice faded away.

'Yes?' said Emma. But he was not saying.

'I think all I can say is that it is a production slip, and that it comes from the factory.'

'Well thank you,' said Emma 'that is most helpful.' She made a note of this, and copied down the main particulars of the document on to her notes. She was careful to take sufficient details to enable her to recognise the document when she was in court, together with the salient details, from her point of view, but without feeling that she had to make a verbatim copy of the whole thing, which would have taken hours.

As with Watsons' documents, it was not easy for Emma to make complete sense of the business records without explanation.

The really instructive part came when she reached the servicing records. At first sight these seemed to be carbon copies of the chits that had been given to her each time the machine had been serviced. She had, of course, brought her documents with her, and quickly found her copies of the servicing chits, for comparison. When she came to compare them, she found that Mr. Richardson (or someone) had completed on Toltons' copy some additional information. There was a space on their copy of each of the three servicing chits which (on their copy only) was headed with the words: 'Remarks'. Here were recorded details of what the mechanic found on his visit to service a machine. These remarks would not appear on the top copy, which the customer received, but only on the copy kept by the firm, as a confidential record of what the mechanic found was wrong with the machine, presumably, and any other relevant remarks not for the eyes and ears of the outside world. Emma made a complete note of what was written on each of the three servicing chits.

On the first one it said: 'Pump u/s due to obsolete bearing? Report to factory for batch check. Adjust b/gm. Free motor'. The next chit included the following in the remarks panel: 'Still vibrates badly, unsuitable belts? Loose m.dr.p and belt damaged. Fit new both.' And the third said: 'Bearing seized up, pump u/s, new not available, call again' and, after a space, '3rd Nov. new pump fixed'.

Emma looked up at Mr. Richardson. 'I take it that these notes here are in your handwriting, Mr. Richardson?' she asked.

'That's right, madam,' he replied.

The rest of the records revealed nothing new. She had already seen the exchange of correspondence between Toltons and Watsons when she had inspected Watsons' documents at Dodds & Son's offices. She had copies of it, indeed, already in her possession, so she needed to do nothing more than check that they tallied exactly. She made a note to this effect.

'Well, thank you,' she said to Mr. Evans. 'I am sorry it has taken me a little time to go through these documents. But I am sure you realise the importance of them to my case. May I hang on to them a little longer, while I discuss with Mr. Richardson the questions I shall put to him in court.'

—getting a statement

Although they were obviously unhappy about discussing his evidence with Emma, they were in fact just as anxious to know what she was going to ask Mr. Richardson as she was anxious to know what he was going to say.

Taking a statement from a potential witness is one of the standard functions of solicitors and policemen. To do it effectively is quite a skilled business, and can be very time consuming. The usual—and probably the best—method is for the person conducting the interview, in this case Emma, to ask the witness a series of questions on the subject, and for the answers to those questions to be written down in the form of a statement from the potential witness, in the first person: 'I then left home and as I was walking along the High Street I saw . . .' This is what Emma did. She started with pure formalities: Mr. Richardson's full name, home address, job, experience, qualifications, general background. Then she dealt with the facts involving her and her washing machine. Then she dealt with the documents, and finally with conclusions. Although both Mr. Evans and Mr. Richardson had said that they could only discuss 'general matters', when it came to it, he came out with a good deal of the history of the matter. This is the statement that Emma finished up with, showing the main points of the evidence that Mr. Richardson would give in her case:

Name: David Henry Richardson; address: 18 Lincoln Park, Setters Green, near Carshalton, Surrey; job: fitter mechanic employed by Toltons Domestic Appliances Ltd; worked for them in that job for about five years. Before that, with Anglo-Belgian Engineering as a fitter in their factory in Reading. Before that, in the army in REME—corporal on leaving the army.

Not apprenticed, but received a full training in basic engineering matters including electrical engineering in the army. 'I would describe myself as a qualified mechanic.'

When joined Toltons, received a period of training at their factory. People joining them as service fitters do a six week course. At the end you have a pretty good idea of most things likely to go wrong with the general range of appliances manufactured by the company. These include dishwashers, spin dryers,

cleaners, grinders, mixers and so on, as well as washing machines; always specialised in home visit
appliances, that is the big machines like washing
machines and dishwashers which have to be dealt
with by visits to the home, rather than being sent to
the service depot.

'In the course of my job, I was called to 14 Twintree Avenue, Minford, in June 1972 to see Mrs.
Seaton. I received a note from the office to call there.
Our job lists are made up in the office at the depot
from phone calls. I cannot remember now what the
trouble was. But looking at the company's copy of
the service sheet for that first visit, I now see that I
noted down at the time that I found that the
machine's pump was u/s, meaning unserviceable, due
to use of obsolete bearing. This would mean that . . .
(witness will elaborate on that in court—won't say
now). The service sheet then refers to a batch check.
This means that the depot were to refer back to the
factory records for a check on whether other samples
of this machine made at about the same time, that is
in the same production batch, were causing trouble or
not. I cannot say whether this was ever done. Sometimes when a modification is introduced to a model,
this causes unforseen difficulties with the early
production models, due to consequence of the modification. Sometimes further modifications are then
introduced to meet the trouble that the first modification caused. Sometimes the first modification is with-
drawn, if the trouble cannot be halted. (Witness
refuses details on this at the moment).

Each time I visited Mrs. Seaton's house, I thought

"Each machine is an individual"

I had corrected the trouble. I cannot say whether this particular machine must have been faulty. Each machine is an individual, you cannot generalise.'

All this took a considerable time to write down, and Emma found that she had been at Toltons' over two hours before her business with them was finished. They too, were surprised at how long it all took. Emma was well satisfied with what she had found out. Both men had been cagey, especially at first, and there were some important aspects of the matter which could only be unveiled when Mr. Richardson would be standing there in the witness box. But she had made some progress. She confirmed with Mr. Richardson once more the arrangements about his attending court on the day of the hearing.

'And don't forget to bring all those papers,' said Emma as she was leaving.

affidavit of service

As Emma had served the witness summons herself—rather than get the court to do so—she had to provide proof to the court that the witness summons had been served. To do so she had to complete and swear the affidavit of service, the form for which had been given to her when she applied for the witness summons. The affidavit had to be filed (that is, left) with the court office within three days after the witness summons had been served. Emma completed the affidavit but did not sign it, and this is how it read when she had finished:

116(2)
Affidavit of Service of
Summons to Witness   In the *Minford* County Court
                No. of Plaint *73/00534*
Between *Mrs. Emma Caroline Seaton*   Plaintiff
     and
Watsons Stores (Minford) Limited   Defendant

    I, *Emma Caroline Seaton* of *14 Twintree Avenue, Minford,* in the County of *Surrey* make oath and say as follows:
    1. That I am *the plaintiff*
                    and that I am over sixteen years of age.
    2. That I did on the *12th* day of *March* 1973 at *349 Godalming Road, Guildford, Surrey* duly serve *David Henry Richardson* of *18 Lincoln Park, Setters Green near Carshalton, Surrey* with a witness summons, a true copy whereof is hereunto annexed, marked 'A', by delivering the same to *him* personally.
    3. That I paid to the said *David Henry Richardson* at the same time the sum of *£2* for his expense (and loss of time).
Sworn at *Minford* in the
County of *Surrey* this
15th day of *March* 19*73*
This Affidavit is filed on behalf of the *plaintiff*.

On the back of her copy of the witness summons, form 116 (1), she wrote 'A—This paper marked A is the copy summons referred to in the annexed affidavit'.

In the court office she signed the affidavit, handed it with the copy of the witness summons to the clerk who checked the papers. He then produced a New Testament and made her swear that 'this is my name and handwriting, and the contents of this my affidavit are true'. There was no fee. He kept the forms.

expert's report

She received from Dodds & Son a copy of Mr. Ardern's report of his findings when inspecting the washing machine on 2 March. The letter from Dodds & Son invited her to agree the report.

REPORT   6th March 1973

on Washfaster washing machine Model No DB 8732/67G

'On the 2nd March I attended at the premises of Mrs. E. C. Seaton, 14 Twintree Avenue, Minford, Surrey to inspect the above machine. The appliance in question had been removed from the place where it had formerly been used and was in the garage, for storage.

In the presence of Mrs. Seaton I examined the said machine and confirmed that a new pump motor had been fitted which was running freely. There was rust on the framework in the vicinity of the pump consistent with it having leaked at some time. The motor shaft was scored and the drive pulley was slightly loose. There was no locking washer on one of the adjustable motor-mounting bolts which was loose and the motor had moved on its bracket allowing the drive belt to slip.

The combined effect of the loose motor mounting and the drive pulley would cause vibration and possibly excessive belt wear. The belt was loose enough on the motor drive-pulley for the drum to run underspeed, at least intermittently and particularly when spinning.

I found that the water inlet filter was badly clogged. I would think it unlikely that this had been cleared since the machine was first installed, and this could result in the tub underfilling.'

Emma studied the report. She did not fully understand it, but as it did not seem to contradict her recollection and impressions, she wrote to Dodds & Son;

> *14 Twintree Avenue,*
> *Minford, Surrey.*
> *17 March 1973*

Dear Sirs

Myself v Watsons

Thank you for your letter of 13 March, enclosing Mr. Ardern's report of 6 March, which I have studied with care. I am quite prepared to accept the accuracy of his findings and I am willing that it should be used in court as an agreed report.

> *Yours faithfully,*
> *Emma Seaton*

Messrs. Dodds & Son.

Agreeing the report meant that Mr. Ardern would not have to attend court, his statement would not have to be proved in court and both parties could refer to it and rely on it in arguing their case.

publicity

One more thing Emma wanted to do was to contact the press. Most cases in the county court are of little interest to the papers. They involve dismal stories of people who are in debt and the same old accident cases. Often no reporters are present. On the whole, reporters spend more time in the magistrates courts, where criminal cases are heard. Emma considered her case to be of some importance to other consumers. The threat of exposure in court was one of the legitimate sanctions she could invoke against a retailer of faulty goods. The only way of letting the press know in advance that the case of Seaton v Watsons might produce some intersting copy for the local press was for Emma to tell them so. She wrote to the editor of the local paper as follows:

> *14 Twintree Avenue,*
> *Minford, Surrey.*
> *23 March 1973*

Dear Sir,

I am writing to tell you about a case that is to be heard at the Minford County Court on wednesday 4 April. In this case, I am the plaintiff, and I am claiming damages from Watsons Stores (Minford) Limited, the department store in Minford High Street. The case concerns a Wash-faster washing machine which I bought from Watsons in May 1972, and which proved to be defective. I am claiming back the price of the machine, plus compensation for expenses and inconvenience.

I am not represented by a solicitor and intend to present my case in court without professional help, as it is quite possible in cases like mine for people to pursue their legal rights in the county court, provided they have enough patience and persistence. I hope to encourage other people to do likewise where they come up against a brick wall (as I did) in pursuing a genuine consumer complaint.

You may feel that it is worthwhile to have a reporter in court when my case is tried (it is expected that my case will begin at about 10.30 am), and to report the hearing in your paper. For further information please phone me at Minford 4974.

Yours faithfully,
Emma Seaton

Arbitration is in private and the press cannot attend, so if you have a consumer case which is referred to arbitration, there is no point in asking a reporter to be present. But you can tell the press about the case.

F

On the day of the hearing Emma checked that she had with her all the papers in connection with the case. She and her husband Matthew arrived at the county court just before 10.30 am, the time at which the court starts sitting. Emma looked around to see if the opposition had arrived. She could see no signs of Mr. Coales from Dodds & Son, the solicitors for Watsons. She looked at the list of cases to be heard that day, pinned up outside the courtroom. It was headed 'Cause list for the 4th April 1973 in Court No. 1, before His Honour Judge Tench'. Three cases were listed for hearing, the last of which was: Seaton v. Watsons—Sale of Goods.

She went to the court office and enquired of the clerk behind the counter whether he knew what time her case was likely to be reached. He said that he had no idea, and that she should ask the clerk of the court. So they crept into the court, which was by now in session. The judge seemed to be listening to a plea from a solicitor for a tenant for an extension of time for leaving a flat. Matthew sat in a pew at the back of the court, and Emma crept as unobtrusively as possible to the front. She approached the clerk of the court, sitting below the judge. She whispered to him: 'My case is Seaton and Watsons. I'm the plaintiff. I'm wondering when it is likely to be on.' He said: 'Might be soon, the way things are going. One case has collapsed already, and this present one won't go on for long. You may be on in half an hour, very likely.' Emma nodded her thanks, and retreated to the back of the court to join her husband. They sat listening to the present case, taking in the atmosphere of the court, and following the procedure. The judge seemed rather reserved, a bit remote, partly due no doubt to his wig and purple gown (the same colour as the cover of this book). Emma shuddered a little at the prospect of his trying her case. But there was no turning back at this stage.

Emma left the court room to see whether her witness, Mr. Richardson, had yet arrived, and whether the opposition had yet put in an appearance. There was no sign of Mr. Richardson in the hall of the court building, and she went outside to see whether he might be standing in the street. He was not. As she came back into the building, she recognised Mr. Coales, the articled clerk from Dodds & Son. In addition, there was a barrister, already bedecked in wig and gown, and two other men, whom Emma did not recognise, but who were presumably from Watsons or their solicitors. Emma was not quite sure whether she ought to greet them or ignore them. She decided on the former, and was about to approach Mr. Coales when he saw her, detached himself from his colleagues and came up to her.

'Good morning,' he said, rather stiffly, as if the presence of his clients inhibited his natural friendliness. 'Could we have a word with you about one or two matters, please?'

'Yes, of course,' replied Emma.

Mr. Coales introduced the barrister who represented Watsons. He was Mr. Keith Sanders, the man whose name appeared at the end of the defence. He was a man in his thirties. The three of them went and sat together in the hall.

offer of settlement

'Well, Mrs. Seaton,' said Mr. Sanders, in a rather haughty way. 'My clients have come here today to fight this case, as you know, and are prepared to do so. My advice to them has been that they have a good defence. But they would be prepared to offer you a settlement, if appropriate terms could be reached. So I'm putting to you an offer, on the basis we call without prejudice. Perhaps you know what that implies, do you?'

'Yes, I know about without prejudice,' said Emma.

'Yes well, since you disdain the employment of solicitors or counsel, madam, it is my duty to explain things to you explicitly. I am sure you understand. The offer I am instructed to put forward is that my clients should give you an allowance of £20 on the washing machine, and that you should keep possession of it, and that each side should bear its own costs in the proceedings. And this would be on the basis of my clients continuing to deny liability.'

'Twenty pounds,' replied Emma 'I can't say that I'm bowled over by your generosity. I feel very disinclined to accept a paltry sum like that, but I will have a word with my husband, if you don't mind, to see what he feels bout it.'

Emma withdrew from the huddle, and walked back to the court room. Just as she reached the door, she noticed that Mr. Richardson was coming into the building. She immediately went up to him and greeted him. He was accompanied by a man who looked as if he had come along to keep an eye on things from Toltons' point of view. So it turned out to be. He was, in fact, from the solicitors for Toltons.

'Ah, Mr. Richardson, thank you for coming,' said Emma. 'You managed to find your way here all right, then.'

'Yes, thank you,' said Mr. Richardson rather formally. 'This is Mr. Hosker from our solicitors.'

'I am pleased you are here, Mr. Hosker, will you just excuse me for a moment. The other side have put an offer to me, which I do not think I can accept, but I just want to discuss it for a moment with my husband.'

Emma left them, and went into the court, extracted Matthew, and had a hasty discussion with him outside the court about the offer of £20 to settle the case. Both agreed that it was not enough, and having gone all this way, and gone to all this trouble, the right thing to do was to reject the offer. If a £20 offer had come when they had first started the case, they would have been interested. Now it was too late. Emma went back to the group containing counsel and the solicitor for Watsons.

'Sorry,' she said. 'We are not interested in £20 at this stage. All or nothing at all, it will have to be.'

'So be it, dear lady,' said counsel, Mr. Sanders. 'Then we must go on.'

the trial begins

Before long, Mr. Coales approached Emma once more. 'We are going into the court now. It looks as if we should be on in about ten minutes, with a bit of luck.' Emma thanked him, and looked at her watch. It was just after eleven o'clock. She collected her papers, and invited Mr. Richardson to join her and Matthew. Mr. Hosker came too. They sat quietly in court, just near the front on the left hand side, which is generally the side for the plaintiff. They listened to the end of the previous case, in which the judge was giving his decision. Just as Emma thought it was over, she found that it was followed by a short argument about costs. Then the lawyers and the parties in the previous case streamed out of the court. Taking her cue from her opponents, Emma moved forward to the front pew on the left hand side of the court room, where there was a table in front of her to put her papers on. There was a subdued hubbub for a little while. Emma noticed that the clerk of the court was having a quiet word with the judge. Then the clerk opened the file in front of him, handed the papers up to the judge, and said in a loud voice: 'Seaton and Watsons Stores (Minford) Ltd'.

This was it. Her case was about to begin.

Emma rose to her feet, trembling a little, and cleared her throat. The hubbub died down. The judge looked at her. She thought for a moment that he was going to speak first, but he did not say anything. So she began: 'In this case, your honour,' she said 'I am the plaintiff, and I appear in person. Mr. Keith Sanders is counsel for the defendants, Watsons Stores (Minford) Ltd. I hope that the fact that I am not represented by counsel or a solicitor will not prove troublesome to the court.' The judge interrupted her, as she paused to collect her thoughts.

'If you are appearing in person in my court,' he said in a kindly way 'it is the custom for you to take

the case from the witness box. Where you are
standing is strictly reserved for members of the legal
profession. However, I observe that there appear to
be a fair number of documents before you, and you
might find it more difficult to deal with them if you
were in the witness box. For my part, I would be
content that you should conduct your own case from
where you are, if counsel has no objection, that is.'

Mr. Sanders rose to his feet. 'I am much obliged to
your honour,' he said. 'We of course have no objection to what your honour proposes, and would not
wish to inconvenience the plaintiff in any way.' He
sat down again.

'Very well, Mrs. Seaton,' said the judge 'you may
conduct the case from there, then, except when you
yourself are giving evidence, when you will go to the
witness box in the usual way. Now, I do not know
how much you know about court procedure. Have
you previous experience of court cases, may I ask?'

'No, your honour,' replied Emma. 'All my knowledge and understanding of courts comes out of a
book, and I trust that your honour will bear with me
if I appear inexperienced in the procedure.'

'Very well,' said the judge. 'We shall have to see
how things go. I shall do what I can, without being in
any way partial one way or the other, to guide you as
to what you may do and may not do. There is a tradition in our courts for the judge to assist litigants in
person within the limits of propriety and I shall follow that tradition in this case, to the best of my abi-
lity. You must not expect, however, that any indul-
gence extended to you in this way will apply to my

decision in the case, which will be purely on the basis of the law and the facts, determined by the evidence. You do understand that, don't you?' he asked.

'I expect no favours, your honour,' said Emma. 'My only hope is that your honour will bear with me if I go astray on questions of law or procedure.'

'Very well,' said the judge. 'Please proceed.'

plaintiff's opening

Emma picked up her copy of the particulars of claim, nervously fingered one or two of the other papers before her, and began. 'I propose first, your honour, to outline the facts of my case. Then I shall go to the witness box and give my evidence. Then I shall call the other evidence—there are two witnesses I propose to call, apart from myself. This case concerns a washing machine which I bought from Watsons Stores in Minford High Street in May 1972. This turned out to be an unfortunate purchase from my point of view, to put it mildly. In essence, this case concerns what went wrong with that washing machine, and whether I am entitled by law to receive my money back from the shop which sold it to me, by reason of certain defects in it. The essential facts are stated in the particulars of claim, and with your permission, your honour, I now propose to read the particulars.' Emma then read the particulars of claim. Then she read Watsons' defence. She continued:

'You will therefore see that the issues in this case are concerned with the state of this particular washing machine at the time it was delivered to my house in May 1972. I say that it was defective; the defendants

in effect deny this, and I am therefore required to
prove it. Before I deal with the documents, I would
like to refer to the law that applies here. This case is
governed by the Sale of Goods Act 1893.'

As I understand it, your honour, and of course I
am no lawyer, the law on the matter comes to this:
the shop which sells something is responsible for
three things: firstly, that the article sold must be reasonably fit for the purpose for which buyers would
intend to use it; secondly, the article must be of merchantable quality; and lastly, the article must correspond with the description by reference to which it
was sold. So far as the purpose for which this washing machine was intended, that is simple. It was
intended to be used for washing clothes, obviously,
and—because of its defects—I say that it was not fit
for that purpose. It only washed clothes intermittently, and from time to time broke down completely.
So far as merchantable quality is concerned, due to
the defects, I say this machine was not merchantable;
that is, a person, knowing of the defects, would not
buy it. And lastly, because it was defective, and
would not consistently wash clothes, I say it was not
really a washing machine at all, and so did not
comply with the description "washing machine",
which is what I asked for, and what the defendants
purported to deliver. On any one of those three
grounds, or any combination of them, I was entitled
to reject the goods when I discovered the true extent
of the defect. This is what I did, and having rejected
the washing machine according to my rights under
the Sale of Goods Act, I now claim the return of the

price I paid for it, namely £84.50. In addition, I claim by way of damages the expenses I incurred by reason of the failure of the machine from time to time, plus compensation for the inconvenience and disappointment that resulted to me. That is the basis of my claim, your honour.'

Emma then turned to the documents. She handed to the judge the three bundles—A, B and C—which had been prepared for him by Dodds & Son and which corresponded with the bundles she had, and which she had agreed with Dodds & Son earlier on. She read out each one, giving an explanation where necessary of any point mentioned in a document which might not be clear. She drew attention to the fact that Watsons' records showed that they had had the machine in stock for over a year before she had bought it. When she came to the agreed report on the washing machine prepared by the expert, Mr. Ardern, she emphasized that the examination had revealed certain defects. She used the documents as a framework on which to explain the whole story of the affair, and by the time she had read the last one, the judge had a fair understanding of what the case was all about, and what the issues were. Emma concluded her opening remarks like this:

'That this machine was defective to some extent can hardly be disputed. If it had never worked at all, or if it had blown up, or something like that, I imagine that there could not have been any dispute about my right, as the buyer, to cancel the purchase and claim my money back, plus damages. If, on the other hand, the machine had worked perfectly well, but I had decided that I did not like the shape or I had felt it was a trifle noisy, then such things would not have been sufficient to justify, as a matter of law, a cancellation of the purchase. This case falls somewhere between those two extremes.

It is therefore a matter of degree, and so largely a question of fact. The law is not soft on shops: what they sell must not be faulty. Is it at all likely that any housewife in Britain would willingly agree to take in satisfaction of a purchase costing £84.50 a washing machine which she knew would break down four times in seven months? The answer must be no, in which case I am entitled to succeed in my claim. Watsons may say that all that was needed in my case was for a mechanic to come along and put it right. But the law does not allow for that. If there is a serious defect, so that after a time an article does not work, the buyer can reject it, get his money back and start all over again—somewhere else, if he likes. He does not have to allow the seller an opportunity of putting right what is wrong, if he does not want to.

What is more, your honour, I say that the position remains the same, even if there is a so called guarantee from the manufacturer, as there was in my case. The manufacturer's guarantee does not affect the contract of purchase. It is an arrangement between the buyer and the manufacturer. It has this significance, however: the buyer of what turns out to be defective goods, on discovering the defect, could—in effect— say to the seller: "Well, this article turns out to be defective, and I therefore have my rights against you, the seller, under the Sale of Goods Act including the right to cancel the purchase, and claim my money back. These rights I now reserve against you. In the meantime, there is this guarantee from the manufacturer, which gives me additional rights regarding putting right defects. Since the whole structure of the trade promotes the idea that it should be the manufacturer who, in practice (never mind the law) puts right defects, I am prepared to go along with that. I will therefore give the manufacturer a chance to honour his guarantee, since in practice that is often the easiest way, maybe the only way, of getting the defects actually put right quickly and effectively, without a legal dispute. But if at the end of the day the manufacturer cannot or will not put right the article, then I will be entitled to revert to my legal rights against you, the seller, and at that point may invoke my right to cancel the purchase." Now, in practice a buyer of a defective article never says that, but that in effect is what he is saying when he claims under a guarantee.

It would be quite unreasonable, bearing in mind the way household appliances are marketed these days, for the buyer to be prejudiced, so far as his rights are concerned, merely because he has allowed the manufacturer an opportunity of honouring his guarantee. So, in conclusion, I say that my right to reject this washing machine, because it was a defective one, was in suspense, so to speak, during such time as I was dealing with Toltons, the manufacturers, and getting them to do what they could to put right the defects in this particular washing machine. After four attempts to get the thing right, all without ultimate success, I then reverted to my legal rights against Watsons. They can hardly complain that I delayed in telling them of what I was experiencing, or in coming to them for redress, for I had in fact been pursuing my problem ever since I bought the machine in the very way that they had laid down at the time of my purchase—that is, through the guarantee. But every reasonable effort on my part to get the matter put right through that channel proved abortive. So in the end I had to activate my legal rights. This I did in my letter to Watsons. From then on, up to this day, the matter has been dealt with according to my legal rights, and it is those that I seek to enforce in this court today.

That is the nature of my claim. Unless there is some further matter which I can explain to your honour, I now propose to begin the evidence, by going myself into the witness box and taking the oath.'

'Thank you, Mrs. Seaton,' said the judge. 'I think you have covered everything, except just this. Take a washing machine which has some small thing wrong with it—say some mechanical connection is not done properly, or something like that, so that it stops working after a short while. Do you say that such a washing machine is not fit for its intended purpose and not of merchantable quality, as provided in the Sale of Goods Act? Even though, let me add, it merely requires a small adjustment or repair, call it what you like, to set it right again?'

'Well, your honour,' said Emma 'my answer to that is that it must depend. I am no lawyer, any more than I am a mechanical or electrical engineer. I suppose there must be a line at which a defect in a washing machine is so trivial that it has to be ignored. But this is not the position in my case. I would suggest that the defects that will be brought out in the evidence you will hear are by no means minimal. And it is surely not the bigness or smallness of the repair which counts. It is the bigness or smallness of the breakdown. If it is a complete breakdown, then surely the machine cannot have been fit for its intended purpose, even though a skilled mechanic has to do very little to put it right again.'

'Yes, I see what you are saying,' said the judge. 'The case may well turn out to revolve round that sort of point. We will no doubt return to it. Let us now begin the evidence.'

evidence in chief

Emma walked to the witness box. The court usher came to the witness box, asked her to take the New Testament (which was kept in the witness box) in her right hand and to read the words on the card. Those who do not hold a religious belief may affirm, rather than take the oath. Some people feel that a witness who affirms is less likely to be believed than one who does the more conventional thing of taking the oath. Whether or not there was any truth in this, Emma did not feel that this was the time to uphold the right to affirm. She read the oath.

'I swear by almighty God that the evidence I shall give shall be the truth, the whole truth and nothing but the truth.' She took pains to make sure that she read the words exactly, without stumbling.

She paused briefly, and then began her evidence. Unlike someone who is represented in court by a lawyer, she had nobody to ask questions of her. This is a snag, because in many ways a person's story comes over more effectively through question and answer. But she was not deterred. She did not hurry, and she did not get flustered.

In giving evidence, a person is allowed to refer to documents which are agreed in advance, or if they have been produced by a previous witness, or by the witness himself, and proved or accepted to be genuine. In addition, a witness is allowed to look at contemporaneous notes to refresh his memory, for example from a diary. It is what the person says which legally constitutes the evidence, even though it is derived from the diary. Not every note or jotting is allowed to be used as a memory refresher in this way. To be eligible, the notes must have been made at the time when the event occured, or so soon after it that the memory of it must have been still fresh in the witness's mind. A delay of a few hours will not matter. The next day may be too late. Thus a diary kept religiously on a day to day basis would usually be all right, but a diary which is only completed once a week, or something like that, is not permitted as a memory refresher. It is important to preserve the original notes one makes at the time of an incident, even if later more coherent notes (even a complete statement) are compiled from the original notes. When it comes to giving evidence in court, a witness can only look at the original notes, no matter how rough.

If you prepare a statement of your evidence, you

are not allowed to read it out loud in court. You have to give your evidence from memory, using only the permitted ways to refresh it.

Emma began her evidence. 'Your honour, my full name is Emma Caroline Seaton, and I live at 14 Twintree Avenue, Minford, Surrey. I am a housewife, and I am married to Matthew John Seaton, who is a company secretary. Before my marriage I was a social worker in the employment of a local authority. I have two children, Daniel aged nine and Josephine aged six.' At this point, the judge asked her to speak a little more slowly, to enable him to make notes of what she was saying. From this point on, she kept her eye on his pen, and only resumed speaking as he finished making a note of what she had just said. There is no shorthand writer in a county court as a rule. She continued her evidence.

'From time to time since we have moved to Minford, I have shopped at Watsons Stores, which is a department store in the High Street in Minford. I have bought small items there, some bed linen, towels, things like that, and some kitchen equipment, but never any major item, until last year. In the early part of 1972 I decided I would get a washing machine. Up until then I had always done the family wash at the launderette or by hand. I began to keep my eye open for something to suit our needs. One day, in May 1972, I was in Watsons buying something else, and I decided to look at their range of washing machines on display. I looked them all over and my attention was caught by a notice on one called a Washfaster, the notice said something like

"Special Offer—£84.50". The price compared well
with what I had seen of other machines, and I asked
an assistant in the shop about the machine. It was a
young lady, I do not know her name. She told me
that the machine was very popular, or something like
that. I think I may have asked her about its capacity
and other matters concerned with the working of the
machine, but so far as I remember she did not
provide much information about that. I asked the girl
in the shop about delivery and installation. She said
delivery would probably be within a week. They had
a fitter who would instal it and get it going for me,
and this was included in the price.

So it was all arranged there and then. The girl took
my order and I paid the £84.50 by cheque.'

Emma described the sequence of events regarding
the delivery and working of the machine—how it
seemed to work all right at first, but then things
started to go wrong. She described the breakdowns,
and the time it took for the man from Toltons to
come each time. She described the frustration she suffered each time this happened, and the trouble and
expense of having to use the launderette. At one point
she said: 'By this time I was getting really fed up with
the thing. I was telling my mother about it on the
phone one day and she said to me . . .'

At this point the judge interrupted her. 'What your
mother, or anyone else for that matter said to you on
the phone, is not evidence, I am afraid. It is what we
call hearsay. If your mother has personal experience
of some aspect of this matter, and you want to put
that in evidence, then she must come here and tell us

what she saw and heard. You cannot tell us what she says she saw and heard. That is not allowed. I am bound to add, Mrs. Seaton, that it does not sound as if what your mother said to you on the phone is relevant, either, and that is another reason for not permitting you to tell us about it. Please continue.'

Emma apologised for her slight transgression of the rules, and resumed her story. She made a point of explaining as precisely as she could, within the limitation of her memory and her technical knowledge, what it was that seemed to go wrong with the washing machine each time it failed, and precisely what the effect was. She described the visits made by Mr. Richardson.

She ended up by saying: 'So when it broke down for the fourth time, and there was all this water all over the floor, I literally burst into tears, I was so frustrated and fed up. I ended up by writing to Watsons on 11th December—the letter I wrote is No 1 in bundle A. I have already read that to you, your honour, and the story from that point on is, I think revealed by the documents. I suppose I should just say, to put it on record, that the letters that I read to the court when I described the case earlier on were in fact written and received by me. Since I did not seem to be getting anywhere by writing letters, I was left with no alternative but to issue a summons in this court, which I then did. Some time after the pre-trial review, the engineer instructed by Watsons came to my house to inspect the machine. Subsequently I received a copy of his report. Your honour has a copy of it.

In conclusion, your honour, it was the frequency of

the breakdowns—four times in eight months—which finally goaded me into cancelling my purchase, plus the "couldn't care less" attitude of Toltons, who were meant to be servicing it for me under their guarantee. If only they had shown some willingness to help me, or even to tell me when I might expect to get it put right, I would not have minded so much. It was the not knowing which caused me so much frustration and distress. It really did upset me. And for this frustration, distress and upset, as well as for my natural disappointment in getting a bad buy, not to mention the loss of use, I now claim compensation. Thank you, your honour.'

cross-examination

Next came cross-examination by the other side. Emma had to stay where she was and wait for the first question from counsel for Watsons. There was a brief pause while the judge, and counsel, finished making a note of her last remarks. Then, realising that she had finished, the judge looked from her towards the barrister, and said: 'Yes, Mr. Sanders.'

Mr. Sanders rose to his feet, took his notes into his hand and began his cross-examination: 'Mrs. Seaton, there are four of you in the family, is that right? Yourself, your husband and your two children?'

'That is correct.'

'And I dare say that you are pretty fussy about how often everyone has clean clothes around the family, aren't you?'

'Well, no different from most mothers, I suppose.'

'But you like to make sure that they all get clean

clothes regularly, don't you?'

'Certainly.'

'What, twice a week for some items, like socks and vests?'

'Could be. It varies. Depends on many things, like the weather, time of year, and what they have been up to. And of course on the garment.'

'Anyway, between the four of you, a good deal of washing is generated each week, isn't it?'

Emma began to sense what he was driving at. 'Quite a lot yes. On average in the last twelve months I would do the washing twice a week. Sometimes more, sometimes less. Not nearly as much washing, I should add, as when the children were babies. Then it was nappies every day, several loads sometimes.'

'Several loads, did you say?'

'Yes. You could not get them all into the machine at one go.'

'And which machine would that be, Mrs. Seaton?'

'Well, the machine I used for the washing in those days.'

'But I thought you told his honour that this machine, the one this case is all about, was the first washing machine your family has had. Didn't you?'

Emma resisted the temptation to flare up. She realised how easy it would be to be caught out in a lie, if you had lied, and how over-enthusiasm, exaggeration, or biased description of events can easily land you in an awkward position when giving evidence which is subject to cross-examination. Most people have no idea how difficult it is to lie or to exaggerate, when giving evidence, without being detected. Cross-examination is in fact a powerful and effective weapon for getting at the truth, and the formality of the court room atmosphere, together with the taking of an oath, all help to this end. Emma gave her reply calmly, keeping her cool. 'Ah, no, let me explain. This certainly is the first washing machine we have ever owned. But I have used washing machines before. Firstly, I used to do a certain amount of washing at my mother's house when Daniel was a baby, and we were living near to my parents' place. Then when we moved away from there, when my husband's job changed, we used the launderettes for a long time. That's where the bulk of it was done when my daughter was small.'

'Very well,' said the barrister. 'Let us get back to the situation of your family wash since you bought this machine, the Washfaster, which you bought from my clients, in May 1972. It is right to say, is it not, Mrs. Seaton, that for the greater part of the period from May to October 1972 your washing machine was more or less in daily use?'

'Not daily use, no. Twice a week, as I said.'

'All right, twice a week, then. Every week. Is that right?'

'Yes. Except when we were away, of course. In the summer. And at half-term, in fact. Plus, of course, those periods when the machine had broken down.'

'Yes, I was coming to those, Mrs. Seaton. There were just three occasions I believe that it broke down.'

'No. Four occasions.'

'Well, just one moment. We have to ignore—for

the purpose of the point I am putting to you, you understand—the last occasion, when—as you might say—it finally broke down. There were three occasions, were there not, when the machine, according to you, went wrong and was subsequently put right again? Is that right?'

'Well, if you like. I don't see why you have to ignore the time it finally went wrong, though. It was just the same as the others.'

'Bear with me, one moment, if you will, Mrs. Seaton. Between May and October 1972 there were just three interruptions to your continuous use of the machine, weren't there?'

'Yes.'

'And on average the machine was out of commission for how long on each of those three occasions?'

'On average for those three occasions, let me see ... about ten days I suppose.'

'So that in all, out of those eight months, the machine was out of commission for approximately thirty days, is that right? About one month?'

'Yes.'

'And that means, doesn't it, that it was in working order for the remaining seven months of that period?' Emma hesitated before answering.

'Isn't that right?' he persisted.

'I suppose it must be. But of course towards the end, after the third attempt at repairing it, I never felt that it was going properly. It was never like it had been when I first had it.'

'That may well be,' said counsel, brushing her qualification aside. 'But nevertheless the machine was working, be it perfectly or not quite so perfectly, for seven months out of the eight, before you decided to want a new one.'

The judge intervened. 'No, Mr. Sanders. This plaintiff has never said that she wanted a new one, and it is unfair to the witness to put your question in such a way as to make her liable to accept more than she really does accept. Kindly rephrase the last question.'

'I am sorry, your honour. I did not intend to trap the witness, of course.'

'Of course not,' said the judge.

'Let me put it to you another way, Mrs. Seaton,' said Mr. Sanders. 'Taking the eight months that you were using the washing machine, it was working for seven of those eight months, wasn't it?'

'Yes.'

'And apart from the deterioration in performance you mentioned a moment ago, it did the family wash for you perfectly satisfactorily for seven-eighths of the time during that period, didn't it?'

'Up to a point it did.'

'Never mind about up to a point, madam. It did your washing, didn't it, when it worked?'

'Yes, I have no complaints.'

'No complaints, you say.' Mr. Sanders turned towards the judge. 'Could I ask that your honour should make a particular note of that very important answer. The witness says that she has no complaints about the machine.'

Emma and the judge opened their mouths to speak immediately.

'All right, Mrs. Seaton,' said the judge. 'I know what your are going to say. You may think counsel is trying to put words into your mouth. But I fully accept what I imagine you were about to say to me by way of protest, namely, that you certainly did have some complaints about this washing machine, but that so far as its performance when it was working is concerned, you have no complaints. Is that right?'

'Thank you, your honour. That is right. Of course I complained bitterly when it went wrong. But it worked all right when it worked all right, if you see what I mean.'

Counsel resumed his cross-examination: 'Now let us proceed to another matter. You would not claim to be any kind of an expert on the working of washing machines, would you?'

'No,' said Emma.

'And you were never able to tell whether a breakdown in the operation of your machine was due to some failure of a major component, or merely of some maladjustment in it, were you?'

'I couldn't say.'

'It is not impossible, is it, that a contributory cause to any of the breakdowns you experienced was a child's sock, or something like that, becoming lodged in some vital part?'

'Well, I don't think so. I never was told that this was a cause of any trouble. And anyway I don't recall any occasion when either of the children were missing a sock in the wash,' said Emma.

'The trouble you had with this machine,' continued

counsel 'could have been quickly rectified by a few minor adjustments—for all you knew?'

'Well, it never in fact was.'

'Until the final time you experienced difficulty, you never contacted Watsons about the problem, did you?'

'No. I was pursuing the matter under the guarantee, as it said I should on the literature that came with the machine.'

'But it is right, isn't it, that the first hint you gave to Watsons that there was anything amiss with the machine, was when you peremptorily wrote to them rejecting the machine, and demanding your money back?'

'Yes. But they were the ones who supplied me with the manufacturer's guarantee which told me that the manufacturer would attend to any faults. It was only when that failed that I had to revert to my legal rights to cancel my purchase, and that's when I turned to Watsons.'

'If only you had given them a chance to do so, Watsons might have done what was necessary—perhaps simply a few adjustments—to get rid of the trouble?'

'I don't accept that. If you look at their letter, when I first wrote to them it was quite clear that they were not going to involve themselves in the question of all the trouble I was having. So far as they were concerned, it was the guarantee or nothing. They didn't want to know.'

The cross-examination proceeded, covering a number of other aspects of the story. Although she felt that her story was somewhat dented as a result of questioning of this sort, she kept calm, and never lost her temper. Sometimes she gave full answers to questions, so far as she could. But on the whole she kept her answers short. She resisted the temptation to go off into explanations and qualifications. If the answer was 'yes' she tried to say 'yes', instead of 'yes, but . . .' or 'yes, and . . .'.

Towards the end of the cross-examination, Emma was feeling somewhat uneasy. But she had managed to steady herself and did not become rattled. This is how the cross-examination ended:

'Well, I must put it to you quite bluntly, therefore, Mrs. Seaton, that your version of the history of this particular washing machine had been grossly exaggerated; and that beyond a few trifling troubles, reasonably capable of correction by any competent servicing engineer, there was nothing wrong with the machine either when you bought it, when you purported to reject it, or at this very moment. That must be so, mustn't it?' Counsel sat down, leaving her to answer this last question on her own, so to speak.

'No, I certainly wouldn't agree with that,' she said. 'Not by any means.' She was stalling for time. 'Trifling troubles, that's what you said, I think. That is quite wrong. To me these were substantial troubles, substantial defects. Each time the machine broke down it would not work at all, it was a complete breakdown and the machine became incapable of use. I don't call that trifling. And . . .' Emma decided not to go on. 'Well, that's it, really.'

'Now, Mrs. Seaton,' said the judge. 'that concludes

the cross-examination. Now you have the right to say anything further you want to say arising out of the matters that Mr. Sanders has been asking you about. But you cannot introduce anything new, anything we have not touched on before, on which Mr. Sanders did not cross-examine you. Do you understand?'

'Yes, thank you, your honour,' said Emma. 'There is just one thing I would like to say. It was put to me that I have used the machine for seven eighths of the period I owned it, before it finally broke down, implying, I think, that the washing machine had had a jolly good bashing without trouble for a good period. But I ought to point out that we were away on holiday for two and a half weeks in the summer, and for just over a week at half term so that, if we are totting it up, that was nearly a month when the machine was not being used because we were away. So out of the eight months of so-called use, it would be more correct to say that for six months the machine was working and not seven months. That is the only point I want to make. Thank you, your honour.' The judge smiled at her.

'Now that your evidence is concluded, Mrs. Seaton, please return to your place at the front of the court. But let us now adjourn for lunch, if that is convenient for you. You may call your next witness immediately after the adjournment. We will resume at 2.15.'

The judge rose, and everyone in court rose in courtesy to him. Emma and Matthew discussed how they thought things were going. Emma had a word with Mr. Richardson and his attendant solicitor. They made a point of not having lunch together. It might be slightly embarrassing for one thing. For another, they did not wish to give the appearance of priming their witness. So Emma and Matthew went one way, and the others went another.

next witness

They were back in court in good time for the resumption at 2.15. As soon as the judge had returned to court and taken his seat, he said to Emma: 'Let us hear from your next witness.'

She said: 'I would like to call my husband, Matthew Seaton.'

Matthew rose from where he was sitting alongside Emma, walked to the witness box and took the oath, with the assistance of the usher, just as Emma had done. Emma then began to ask him questions, assuming again the role of her own advocate. It did feel rather odd asking her own husband questions to which she obviously knew the answers. But although she was asking the questions, the answers were intended for the judge.

'What is your full name?'

'Matthew John Seaton.'

'And where do you live?'

'Fourteen Twintree Avenue, Minford.'

'And what is your occupation?'

'I am a company secretary.'

'Are you my husband?'

'I am.' They smiled, slightly embarrassed at this revelation.

'Did we buy a washing machine in May 1972 . . .'

Mr. Sanders was on his feet in a flash. 'I must object to that question, your honour. The plaintiff must not ask leading questions.'

'Well, I know,' said the judge. 'But this is a litigant in person, Mr. Sanders, so we should not expect the same standards of conduct in examining a witness as we expect of members of the bar. And even then, Mrs. Seaton was asking the witness about matters which are not really in dispute, so I think I would have allowed the question anyway.' The judge now turned to Emma to explain. 'Counsel has objected, Mrs. Seaton, on the grounds that the question you put to your husband is a leading question. That is to say, it is a question which itself suggests the answer you expect to get. You said, if I remember rightly, "did we buy a washing machine last May?" Now, putting a question that way is not usually allowed when you are examining your own witness. It is all right when you are cross-examining a witness from the other side, and Mr. Sanders put numerous leading questions when he cross-examined you before lunch. But when you are examining your own witness, as you now are, leading questions cannot be asked. Instead, you should have said: "Is there a washing machine in your house? When was it bought? What type is it? Who bought it?"—and so on. Put like that, the witness has to provide the information from his memory. Do you follow? In the formal, or non-controversial parts of a witness's evidence, however, leading questions are often asked without objection. Now I do not expect you to follow the rules as thoroughly as if you were learned counsel. But will you try to avoid leading questions?'

'I will do my best, and I apologise,' said Emma. 'Now let me try again. Mr. Seaton, is there a washing machine in our house?'

'Yes there is.'

'Will you tell the court about how it came to be there?'

'Yes, well, you bought it last May. I understand you bought it from . . .'

'Let me stop you there . . .' said Emma, with a straight face. 'Do you know of your own knowledge where it was bought, or only from what you have heard from someone else?'

'Only from what I have heard from you.'

'In that case you cannot give evidence about it. Confine your answers to things you know from your own knowledge. Now, have you seen this washing machine in action?'

'Yes, quite often. At weekends mainly.'

'And have you seen it not working?'

'Yes, it broke down four times altogether. I was at home on one of those occasions. But on the other occasions, acting on information received'—this brought a smile in the courtroom—'I examined the machine and found that it was not working properly.'

'Yes. And will you state please what went wrong, so far as you could judge, each time you examined it.'

'Yes. The first time it went wrong was, I think, about a week or ten days after it was delivered . . .' Matthew explained what he had found. In doing so he was mainly confirming the evidence that Emma had given about the breakdowns in the machine. It was helpful to have this corroboration. Even though a husband is obviously a biased source, his evidence is well worth having. Corroboration is often very valuable. Of course, it is better still if it can be produced from an independent witness.

It was not necessary to take Matthew through the whole story again, but only those parts which were likely to be disputed. It took only a few minutes for him to give his evidence in chief.

He was then cross-examined by Mr. Sanders, counsel for Watsons.

'You weren't there when these breakdowns took place, were you? You were at work?' asked counsel.

'That's right. But at least one of them took place at a weekend when I was there.'

'So you cannot say what the cause might be?'

'The cause? That's another matter altogether. Are you suggesting that because I was not there, the breakdowns might not have happened at all?'

'You must not start asking me questions,' said Mr. Sanders rather haughtily. 'The point of my question is this. You cannot relate what happened at the time of a breakdown, except the one that occurred when you were at home. From your own knowledge, that is. Is that right?'

'I would agree with that.'

There was no need for re-examination after Matthew had been cross-examined. In other words, there were no questions which Emma felt she had to ask Matthew arising out of matters which had been asked by Mr. Sanders. Matthew now left the witness box.

the last witness

'I now call Mr. David Richardson,' said Emma. She looked around and indicated to Mr. Richardson, sitting behind her, that he should now go into the witness box, taking his documents with him. Mr. Richardson took the oath. Emma picked up the statement she had taken from him on the day that he had been served with the witness summons, and began to ask him questions. After asking his name, address, and details of his job and of his experience, she moved to the crucial description of what Mr. Richardson had found when he first came to repair her washing machine.

'What did you find?' she asked.

'I couldn't rightly say at this distance of time,' he replied.

'Is it your practice to make a note of what you do when you visit someone's house to do a job?'

'Yes. I make a note on a job ticket, as we call it.'

'And is there a copy of that made?'

'Yes. The customer gets the copy as a servicing invoice.'

'And is the copy the customer gets exactly the same as the copy kept by you?'

'No.'

'What is the difference?'

'On our copy are the details of the job done.'

'If you were to look at your firm's copy, that is the job ticket, for the visits you made to my house, would you find there details of the jobs you did to my washing machine?'

'I should do.'

'And have you brought them with you to-day to this court, as required in the witness summons I served upon you?'

'I have them here,' said Mr. Richardson. He rummaged for a little; as he was doing so Emma explained the situation to the judge.

'These were some of the documents I asked this witness to produce, your honour, and I shall suggest that he will be entitled to refresh his memory as to the work he did on my machine by looking at those job tickets.' The judge agreed that this would be allowed, provided that it was proved that the job tickets were contemporaneous notes made by Mr. Richardson himself. This was the first thing that Emma asked him, as soon as he found them and put them in front of him.

'Do those documents now in front of you show details of the work you did to my machine?' she asked him.

'They do.'

'And were the details shown there filled in by you, with your own hand?'

'That's right.'

'When was that done?'

'As soon as the job was done, before I left the house. That's what we always do.'

The foundation was now laid for Mr. Richardson to look at the documents, and to give evidence about what had been wrong with the washing machine on each of the three occasions when he had visited Emma's house.

'Very well,' said Emma. 'Now will you tell the

court what it was you found wrong with the machine
on each occasion that you visited my house, the date
of the visit, and what you did. Will you speak slowly,
Mr. Richardson, to give his honour a chance to make
a note of what you say.'

'The first visit was on the fifth of June. The pump
was not operating so I adjusted the bearing
mountings and freed up the motor and the machine
was left in working order. I noted that there were
obsolete bearings in the pump and recommended that
a batch check should be made.

The second visit followed a report from the
customer of a rumbling noise when the washing
action started. I found this was due to the motor drive
pulley working loose. This had damaged the pulley
and frayed the drive belt. I replaced these parts and
left the machine working correctly.' Emma interrupted him. 'And what was the date, Mr. Richardson?' she asked. 'August the 11th,' he said. 'The
third time was on the 31st of October. On that
visit I found that the pump was not working because a bearing had seized up. I did not carry a
suitable spare pump so I had to leave the machine
faulty but went a few days later with a replacement pump which I fitted. Also a clip on the pump had
come loose, which I tightened as best I could.'

Emma next focussed attention on the condition of
the washing machine when Mr. Richardson saw it
after the first breakdown. 'Looking at the record of
what you did on that first visit on the 5th of June 1972
and your memory of it, can you say what the exact
cause of the breakdown was?'

'Well, not exactly,' said Mr. Richardson, evading the point of the question. 'Could be a number of things, really.'

'Such as?'

'Well the pump mountings may have got displaced slightly in transit or when the machine was being installed or the pump might have been misaligned when it was assembled. The bearings are now obsolete and they have been replaced with self-aligning bearings which cannot give the same sort of trouble.'

'From your experience as a service mechanic, doing this sort of work every day, would you say this sort of breakdown is quite common with the Washfaster model?' asked Emma, probing cautiously.

'It happens. I've seen this sort of thing before, and I'll no doubt see it again. But not all that frequently.'

'How could it have happened that this machine came to have that sort of trouble within two weeks or so of it having been delivered new?' she asked.

'Well, it is not for me to say.' Emma had to frame her questions with care. Mr. Richardson was managing to avoid answering her more awkward questions, but you are not allowed to cross-examine your own witness, as a rule.

'Bearing in mind how often you have seen this sort of trouble with other samples of this model, was it likely that the cause of the trouble was something that happened to the machine after it was installed?' This was the key question.

'Not really.'

'Turning your attention to the other two breakdowns which took place, and which you came to remedy, could they have been caused by things which happened after the machine was installed?'

'Well, the longer it is that a machine has been in use, the more difficult it is to establish what was the underlying cause of the trouble. I do not know what housewives get up to. Some of the things I find when I go into people's houses would astonish you. Some people treat their appliances something cruel. You'd scarcely credit . . .'

'Forgive my interrupting, but will you confine your answers to the particular washing machine in question. Could its second and third breakdowns—you can see the details from the job tickets in front of you—could they have occurred through things that happened after the washing machine was installed?'

'Well, it's possible,' he said, still hedging.

'Is it likely?' said Emma.

'No. It's not likely,' said Mr. Richardson.

'You last saw this machine when?' she asked.

He looked at the job tickets, and found the last one. 'That was on the 3rd of November last.'

'And you have not seen it since?'

'No.'

'Thank you,' said Emma, and sat down.

Mr. Richardson was then cross-examined by counsel for Watsons. 'How long did it take you to put right whatever was wrong with the washing machine on that first visit?' he asked.

'Oh, about fifteen minutes, I would say.'

'It was quite a simple job, then,' said counsel.

'Oh yes, not difficult.'

'A matter of routine to someone skilled and experienced at it like you?'

'Certainly.'

'Although to a layman perhaps an impossible or difficult task?'

'I would say so. You've got to know what you're doing when you take these machines apart.'

'I am much obliged. They are complicated machines, are they not?'

'Comparatively speaking, they are, yes, sir.'

'And would I be right in thinking that the tiniest little thing being not quite right can throw the whole thing out, so that it stops working?'

'That's quite often the case.'

'And yet just quarter of an hour's work from you, a bit of adjustment here and there, and off she goes again, as good as new. Is that right?'

'Yes, sir.'

'And would it be right to say that, as often as not, what you are doing to the machine is more by way of maintenance than repair.'

'Well, I have to cope with both, sir, as part of my job. It's frequently six of one and half a dozen of the other.'

'And a washing machine, like any other machine, needs maintenance, adjustment and attention from time to time, does it not?' said counsel.

'Perfectly true, sir. And the public often don't appreciate the fact, and neglect their appliances rather badly, sir.'

Counsel sat down, well satisfied with these answers, which had given the impression (although that is not what the witness had said) that in this parti-

cular case the work on Emma's machine had been—
in part at least—maintenance, rather than repair following a breakdown. Emma needed to correct this
impression and therefore re-examined Mr. Richardson.

'You told counsel that washing machines need
maintenance and adjustment from time to time, and
that often what you do when you come to people's
homes is to do that.'

'Yes.'

'Casting your mind back to the visits you paid to
my house, and looking at the job tickets for those
visits—take them into your hand, would you,
please—was the work you did to my machine by way
of maintenance only, or did you carry out any
repairs?' she asked. There was a longish pause.

'Some maintenance, and repairs,' he said. Emma
sat down.

The judge thanked Mr. Richardson and he left the
witness box. Emma rose to her feet once more and
addressed the judge. 'That is my case, your honour,'
she said, and sat down.

the case for the defendant

Mr. Sanders, counsel for Watsons, now rose to his
feet, to open his case, that is, to explain to the judge
the general nature of the case for the defence. He
might have argued there and then that the defence had
no case to answer. The defence may say, for instance,
that the evidence produced for the plaintiff does not
prove that which the plaintiff alleged in his particulars
of claim actually happened.

There could also be a submission of no case to

answer where a point of law is involved. The defendant may, in effect, say that legally he is not liable as claimed, even if all the plaintiff's evidence is true.

It is unusual, however, for there to be a submission of no case to answer. The normal procedure is that the case is opened for the defence and then witnesses for the defence are called. This is what happened in Emma's case.

Mr. Sanders opened the case for the defence at some length. 'We say that this is a storm in a tea-cup, your honour,' he began. 'In my submission the plaintiff's claim has been exaggerated beyond all reasonable measure, and shows a complete misunderstanding about the nature and extent of the responsibility of a retailer for the goods he sells, under modern conditions. The plaintiff had some trouble with her washing machine, certainly. That cannot be denied. But what does it amount to? Not very much, in my submission. It stopped working on three occasions, and on the fourth it spilled some water on to the floor of her kitchen. That, I submit, is not enough to entitle a buyer to reject goods out of hand, as this plaintiff purported to do. On the evidence I shall hope to show that—even considering the faults as being as serious as the plaintiff makes out—there is no breach of condition covered by the provisions of the Sale of Goods Act sufficient to entitle the plaintiff to reject the goods and demand the return of the price. That brings me straight away to an examination of the provisions of sections 13 and 14 of the Sale of Goods Act, your honour, and I propose to direct your honour's attention to those sections now.' Mr. Sanders took up one of the hefty legal tomes that he had brought with him to court, opened it at a page which had a slip of paper marking the place, and made ready to read it. The judge also had a pile of legal books beside him, and took one of them and opened it.

'You don't have a copy of the Act, the Sale of Goods Act 1893, that is, do you, Mrs. Seaton?' the judge asked Emma.

'No, your honour, I'm afraid I do not.'

'And presumably you do not have the law reports which Mr. Sanders intends to refer to. He told my clerk in advance, but as you were not legally represented presumably you have not been notified. Well, never mind. You will have to do your best to follow what the argument is.'

Mr. Sanders read out the sections of the Sale of Goods Act which impose obligations on the seller about the quality and fitness for purpose of goods.

Mr. Sanders then continued: 'The plaintiff seems to have presented her case to this court on the basis that the seller is always responsible for all faults in goods, including appliances, come what may. But as your honour will understand, it is not in law quite so simple as that. The law breaks down the obligations of a seller under the act into three kinds, and imposes on the seller obligations which vary according to the circumstances: these are a duty to provide goods which comply with the description under which they were sold; a duty, subject to some exceptions, one at least of which is important in this case, to provide goods which are reasonably fit for their intended purpose; and lastly, a duty to provide goods which are of merchantable quality. I would now like to distinguish

Emma was soon lost . . .

these three obligations and to analyse the extent to which they apply to this case.'

Mr. Sanders then proceeded to dissect the exact words that appear in the sections of the Sale of Goods Act. Emma was soon lost. Before long, Mr. Sanders started to refer to various reported legal cases, where these sections had been considered by High Court and Appeal Court judges in the past. Some decisions of the House of Lords were also quoted. The judge intervened from time to time, and took issue with counsel on various points. Emma was a little alarmed to find that there seemed some room for doubt about what the Sale of Goods Act meant. She had thought that such fundamental and far-reaching law must have been considered and applied to thousands of similar cases in the courts in the past, so that everyone would know just how it applied to cases of faulty appliances. This did not seem to be so. But the judge seemed well able to counter the arguments put by counsel, and by the end of Mr. Sanders' opening, Emma had the clear impression that the judge did not accept the argument put by counsel that Watsons were not legally responsible for what happened to the washing machine.

witness for defence

'I will now call my evidence, your honour,' said counsel. 'Call Kenneth James Hurst.'

Mr. Hurst, the sales manager at Watsons, went to the witness box, took the oath and gave details of his position and experience with Watsons. 'There is no dispute about this, but we may as well get this clear,' said counsel, 'did your company sell a Washfaster washing machine to the plaintiff, Mrs. Emma Seaton, in May 1972?'

'That's right,' said Mr. Hurst.

'And did your company arrange for the washing machine to be installed at Mrs. Seaton's house in Minford?'

'That is so.'

'And in what month would that have been?'

'That was also in May 1972.'

'And was there any complaint from the buyer at the time about the machine?'

'No, none.'

'Or about the manner of the installation, or anything of that kind?'

'No, no complaint whatsoever.'

'If you please. And what was the first you knew of any complaint?'

'It was when we received a letter from Mrs. Seaton asking us, or rather telling us, to take back the washing machine and refund the money she had paid for it.'

'And when was that—look through the pile of letters there, Mr. Hurst, would you, and see if you can find the letter.'

'Yes, here it is' said Mr. Hurst. 'It was dated 11th December 1972.'

'So there was not a word from Mrs. Seaton to your company about this unfortunate washing machine from the beginning of May to the middle of December?'

'That is right.'

And so on. The implication of this evidence was that Emma's problems with the machine were trifling, and that if they had been substantial, Watsons would have heard of it sooner than they did. Mr. Hurst's examination by Mr. Sanders ended like this:

COUNSEL: Present-day electrical appliances are complicated pieces of machinery, would you say?

HURST: Yes, and delicate, too. A modern automatic washing machine contains a control mechanism which is finely balanced and needs adjustment from time to time.

COUNSEL: In your experience, do machines such as the one that Mrs. Seaton bought need adjustment from time to time?

HURST: They certainly do.

COUNSEL: And is it possible, would you say, for a machine to do its job perfectly well once it had been adjusted?

HURST: I agree.

COUNSEL: And be saleable as a washing machine?

HURST: Yes.

COUNSEL: And in fact still correspond with the description 'washing machine', although it may need some adjustment to make it work perfectly again?

HURST: That would be so.

COUNSEL: To what extent, would you say from your experience, do washing machines and similar complicated domestic appliances have minor teething troubles for a while after they are delivered new?

HURST: Very common.

COUNSEL: And what provision is normally made for dealing with such troubles?

HURST: It varies. In some cases, as with Toltons' Washfaster, the manufacturers do the after sales servicing so that we do not come into it. In other cases—particularly portable appliances like toasters, food mixers, radios and so forth—the goods come back to us and we have them serviced by the manufacturers.

COUNSEL: And who pays?

HURST: Well, in all these sort of cases there is a manufacturer's guarantee, or in the case of imported appliances, usually the main agent or importers arrange the servicing, something like that.

COUNSEL: Is a breakdown in the early period of ownership of a complicated electrical appliance something that consumers have come to expect?

HURST: Well, I don't think people are surprised when it happens to them, put it that way.

COUNSEL: And are consumers generally satisfied when the problems, such as they are, can be put right under the guarantee, as you have just described?

HURST: I would say so, yes.

The judge now intervened.

JUDGE: Just let me get it clear what you are saying, Mr. Hurst. Are you saying that people who buy washing machines ought to expect them to go wrong, because they nearly always do?

HURST: No, sir, I'm not saying that. But if there are problems in new equipment, then people are generally happy about the system under which they get them put right.

JUDGE: That may well be so. But there shouldn't be faults there in the first place, should there? All you are saying really is that these days things go wrong with new appliances so frequently that people aren't surprised. That is hardly a matter for congratulation or complacency among those who manufacture and sell them, though, wouldn't you agree?

HURST: Well, we do our best, sir, to help people who have problems.

Mr. Sanders looked discouraged. There was a little more to ask his witness, and shortly afterwards he sat down, leaving Emma to cross-examine Mr. Hurst.

EMMA: You told the court about guarantees for new domestic appliances. The Washfaster your shop sold me had a guarantee, didn't it?

HURST: Yes, I believe it did.

EMMA: Would you look at it, please. It is among the pile of original documents. Can the witness be shown it please?

The clerk of the court handed the original guarantee to Mr. Hurst.

EMMA: That is it, isn't it?

HURST: It would seem so.

EMMA: That guarantee came with the washing machine, together with the instructions. Would you accept that?

HURST: Certainly. That is the usual practice.

EMMA: Your shop sent the guarantee with the washing machine, didn't it?

HURST: Yes.

EMMA: So if I took up complaints about the washing machine in accordance with what it said on the guarantee, that would be acting in accordance with what your shop had stipulated, by providing the guarantee with the machine, isn't that right?

HURST: Well yes, I suppose so.

EMMA: And you expect buyers of things to take up faults under the guarantee, don't you? That is the usual form?

HURST: As a rule, except where, as I mentioned earlier, things get brought back to us. Small things.

EMMA: But you couldn't do that with a washing machine, could you?

HURST: No.

EMMA: The point I am putting to you, Mr. Hurst, is that you don't expect to hear of complaints about a washing machine, do you? It will be attended to under the guarantee, won't it?

HURST: Well, not always. People do complain to us direct sometimes.

EMMA: Oh really? And what do you tell them then?

HURST: Well, we look into it. And . . . do what we can.

EMMA: You refer them to the guarantee, surely, don't you? You tell them to take the matter up with the manufacturers, under the guarantee that came with the machine, when you delivered it?

HURST: Yes. That would be right in most cases.

EMMA: Exactly. So that if you heard nothing from a buyer who was having trouble with a washing machine, he or she could be taking up the matter actively under the guarantee, and dealing direct with the manufacturer, just as you intended. Isn't that so?

HURST: Could be.

EMMA: And is there the slightest reason you can think of why a buyer in that situation should get in touch with you to tell you what was happening?

HURST: None that I can think of.

EMMA: There is nothing about doing that on the guarantee itself, is there?

HURST: I have never heard of one that did.

EMMA: Quite. So the fact that you have heard nothing from a buyer of a washing machine does not mean necessarily that she hasn't had trouble with it, does it?

HURST: I suppose not. I hadn't thought of it that way, really.

EMMA: But you do appreciate, don't you Mr. Hurst, that the legal responsibility for faults in goods lies with the shop which sold it?

HURST: So I understand. But in practice it does not work out like that. Not very often, anyway. We regard it as being the manufacturer's responsibility.

EMMA: Really? Well, that is not how the law regards it. If a manufacturer fails to give satisfaction under the guarantee, surely it is the most appropriate thing for the buyer then to turn to the retailer, claiming in accordance with the Sale of Goods Act?

HURST: Possibly. But I would have thought that it would be sensible to give the shop a chance to use its good offices to help sort out the problem, rather than weigh in with a cancellation straight away.

EMMA: Will you look at the letter you wrote on the 14th of December 1972 to me, in reply to my letter cancelling the purchase. Read it out loud will you, Mr. Hurst?

HURST: (does so)

EMMA: Now, in the face of that, are you saying that you would have said anything different to me if I had written to you saying 'please I am having trouble with my washing machine—could you help to sort it out?' You would have written almost the same letter, wouldn't you?

HURST: I don't know about that.

EMMA: Look at Mr. Ardern's report. Have you seen that before?

HURST: I have read a copy.

EMMA: You are familiar with its contents.

HURST: More or less.

EMMA: There is nothing there which contradicts what I have said in evidence about the four occasions the machine broke down, is there?

HURST: I am not a technical expert. I cannot say.

EMMA: Well, neither am I, Mr. Hurst. But it is obvious even to a layman, isn't it, that there must have been something, for it to have gone wrong in the way described?

HURST: Not necessarily. I find that people do most extraordinary things with their appliances. I have heard of cases where the trouble has been that the machine has not been plugged in. Things like that.

EMMA: Are you suggesting that this might have been the trouble in my case, Mr. Hurst?

HURST: That's not what I said.

EMMA: Do you accept the fact that my machine did break down four times as I have described it in court here today?

HURST: Well, I wasn't there, was I?

EMMA: You don't accept it, then?

HURST: I am not calling you a liar, madam, please don't think that. I have seen and heard of so many things that people do to abuse their things, that I cannot just blindly accept what people say about the troubles they have with their machines.

And on that slightly unsatisfactory note (unsatisfactory from Emma's point of view) she ended the cross-examination.

Mr. Sanders rose once again to say: 'That is my case, your honour.' So, Mr. Hurst was after all the only witness for the defence. This was no surprise, as the only other witness likely to have been called for the defence was the technical expert, Mr. Ardern. Since his report had been agreed by both sides, there was no need for him to be called. The registrar had urged both sides at the pre-trial review to agree the technical report, in order to save the considerable expense involved in asking experts to turn up to give evidence.

final address

Having called his witness, and then closed his case, Mr. Sanders could then address the judge once again. He did so, but quite shortly, as most of his argument had been put to the court in opening the case shortly before. There was little for him to add now. Repetition tends to reduce the effectiveness of argument.

Conscious of this, no doubt, Mr. Sanders did nothing more than sum up the effect of the evidence of his Mr. Hurst. He finished his final address in these words.

'So what it comes to, your honour, is this. The defendants are not seeking to evade their legal responsibilities in relation to this sale. They fully accept that they have to honour their obligations imposed on them by the Sale of Goods Act 1893, and indeed it is their policy, as we have seen, to go beyond their legal obligations in many instances, and—in the interests of good relations with their customers—to go out of their way to help with getting problems put right with merchandise. With goods that are unused they have been known to take them back even if the customer merely changes her mind about them, which is of course beyond anything laid down in the law regarding their duty to buyers. But in this case, your honour, the situation is quite different. The plaintiff seems to misunderstand not only the policy of my clients, but also the law about sale of goods. The seller is not, under the act, responsible for every fault, however trivial, come what may. Having regard to the evidence about the amount of time and effort that was required to put right such defects as there were in this machine, in my submission the plaintiff has failed to establish that this machine was not of merchantable quality. On these grounds, I ask for judgment for the defendants, and that this claim should be dismissed with costs.'

Mr. Sanders sat down.

Emma's final address

Emma rose to her feet to make her final address to the judge. Before she had a chance to say anything to him, he said to her: 'Mrs. Seaton, I do not think I shall need to trouble you, except just on one point.' These words meant, in effect, that she had all but won her case. If, when the time comes for the final submission by or on behalf of the plaintiff, the judge has already made up his mind in favour of the plaintiff, then obviously he does not need to spend more time listening to argument to support a decision in favour of the plaintiff. But there was one point on which the judge wished to hear Emma put her argument. 'The only point that I am undecided about is the question of time. Under the Sale of Goods Act the buyer loses the right to reject goods that are faulty, once he has accepted them. You purported to reject this washing machine—or to cancel your purchase, as you put it—some seven months after the purchase. Do you say that you had not accepted your washing machine, in the legal sense of that word, by December 1972, having bought it the previous May? Have you anything to say on that question?'

'Well, your honour, I will try,' said Emma. 'Not being a lawyer, I cannot claim to master all the underlying legal principles, or to be able to place before you an analysis of the court decisions, in the way that counsel for the defendant has done. All I can do is to apply common sense to the words in the act. As I understand it, the problem comes to this. The law requires the buyer to reject faulty goods within a reasonable time and the buyer is taken to have accepted the goods—and so lost his right to reject them—if, after the lapse of a reasonable time, he retains them without telling the buyer that he has rejected them. So it all depends on what is a reasonable time in the circumstances. This must vary enormously, depending on the facts. In my case, the seller stipulated that faults were not to be dealt with through him but by direct contact with the manufacturer. So long, therefore, as I was dealing with the manufacturer in the hope and expectation that he would correct the faults which had shown up, surely I cannot have forfeited my legal right to reject the goods. It would make nonsense of the law if, by doing the very thing which the seller required me to do about faults, I lost my main redress against the seller regarding those faults. One has to assume that people are reasonable and behave in a rational, common sense way, in the real world of the present day. Would it not be fanciful to suppose that a buyer of a washing machine, would, as soon as she discovers a fault, rush back to the seller and say: "I reject this. I want my money back." What the reasonable person says is: "There is this fault. Would you like to try and put it right?" It would be ridiculous if the law were to require you first to be unreasonable—that is requiring you to reject faulty goods immediately—before you are reasonable, that is, allowing an opportunity to put right the faults. I suppose my case in law would have been that much stronger if I had written to Watsons forthwith on that very first occasion when my machine went wrong, and said: "I reject this horrible washing machine, and require you to pay my money back here and now." Would that have been reasonable? Is that what retailers and manufacturers expect their customers to do? Instead of doing that, I allowed the retailer and the manufacturer, between them, a fair chance to put right what was wrong. Given the facts of this case, the succession of breakdowns, the stop-go history of this machine, I suggest that seven months was by no means too long and that while I was going along with Watsons' way of correcting faults—that is, through the manufacturers under the guarantee—my right to reject the goods was in suspense. After giving a fair opportunity to correct the faults, but to no avail, in December I invoked my right to reject. On each occasion when the washing machine broke down, I acted promptly. I phoned the manufacturers immediately on each occasion, to ask them to come and correct the faults. On every single occasion when a fault came to my notice I sought redress as soon as I could. And when at last I came to the realisation that this machine was faulty beyond the apparent capacity of the manufacturers to repair under the guarantee, then—and without delay—I invoked my right to reject the machine. I therefore say that this was done within what the law defines as a reasonable time in the circumstances, and was not too late.'

judgment
'Very well, Mrs. Seaton. Thank you very much.' Emma sat down. The judge paused, and glanced back through his notes. He then began to give judgment, that is, his decision in the case. This is what he said:

'In this case, the plaintiff, Mrs. Emma Seaton, who has conducted her case with considerable skill and confidence, claims the return of the price paid, plus damages for breach of contract, in regard to a Wash-faster washing machine which she bought from the defendants, Watsons Stores (Minford) Ltd, in May 1972. It has not been suggested—nor could it be—that the defendants themselves were in any way to blame for what went wrong with the washing machine which Mrs. Seaton bought. They were from a prac-tical point of view just intermediaries, having bought the machine from its manufacturers, Toltons Domestic Appliances Ltd, in the normal way of trade. This case has been contested between the plaintiff and the defendants purely on the basis of the contract of sale, bearing in mind that in law the seller is respon-sible for the condition of the goods which he sells. There are implied into the contract of sale certain conditions as to quality and fitness for purpose, by virtue of sections 13 and 14 of the Sale of Goods Act 1893, and this case turns on the meaning of these statutory conditions. The facts are comparatively simple.'

The judge then went through the basic facts about the purchase. He then came to the troubles that Emma had had with the machine.

'The plaintiff said in evidence that the machine was the source of a great deal of trouble. She said that it broke down on four separate occasions between May 1972, when she bought it, and December 1972, when she purported to reject it. I listened with great atten-tion to what counsel for the defendants said about those breakdowns. He suggested that the plaintiff had exaggerated their significance, and that they were in reality rather trivial matters, readily capable of being put right by adjustment—that was the word used. I do not accept this. I found the plaintiff to be a witness of truth and candour, and I do not think that she exaggerated what happened and what she experienced in regard to this machine. A busy housewife, looking after a family, would find it a very frustrating experience to have a new washing machine break down four times in seven months. I accept that on each of those four occasions something—I do not need to decide what—happened to what I will call the "works" of the washing machine which caused it to stop operating. Each time the failure was serious enough to bring about a complete discontinuance of operation, with the result that on each occasion the plaintiff was faced with calling out the mechanic from Toltons, the manufacturers, to come and put it right. Now, I can well imagine that, if the mechanic from Toltons had been able to visit the plaintiff quickly on each occasion, or even on any occasion, or if the servicing system had been more competent, so that the machine could have been put right swiftly and thoroughly, at a time fixed by appointment on the telephone, Mrs. Seaton would perhaps have been content to keep this machine, and would not have felt the need to invoke her legal rights, and commence these proceedings. It is not really relevant to this case that it was frustration at the apparent indifference and incompetence in the matter of servicing that goaded Mrs. Seaton into action. But at the same time, it does not affect the responsibilities of the defendants, either. Their duty under the contract was to supply a washing machine which was not faulty, and in this they manifestly failed. The fact that they partly passed their responsibilities to the manufacturers who provided a guarantee with the goods they sold does not, in my judgment, absolve them from the seller's responsibilities under the law.

I have given careful consideration to the expert's report and have reached the conclusion that the trouble which Mrs. Seaton experienced with this machine was attributable, in part at least, to the faults described in Mr. Ardern's report. There may have been other matters which could have contributed to the breakdowns that occurred. But it is not for the buyer of defective goods to prove, in proceedings under the Sale of Goods Act, what was the cause of the fault, from a technical point of view. What has to be proved is that there was a serious fault. Now we might have had an interesting debate about how serious is 'serious'. The defendants have pleaded— indeed it is the cornerstone of their case—that what defects there were in the machine were trivial ones. I reject this. If a new washing machine breaks down completely within a short period, say a month or two, of being delivered new, that is prima facie evidence of there being a serious defect in it. In the absence of an alternative explanation of the breakdown of a technical character, perhaps, or of some misuse on the part of the buyer of the machine, or something similar, I am entitled to find, as I do find in this case, that the machine had a serious defect in it.

What does this amount to in law? I put on one side the question of whether a serious defect in a washing machine could fall within section 13 of the Sale of Goods Act, which deals with the description of goods. In other words, I do not find it necessary to decide whether a piece of machinery, having within itself some latent defect which will, before long, cause it to fail, can be described as a washing machine at all. That brings me to consider section 14 of the act. That section comes in two halves. One subsection deals with fitness for purpose. Subject to certain qualifications it is provided that on a sale of goods by a person in the course of business, there is an implied condition that the goods are reasonably fit for their intended purpose. Having regard to the latent defects that were in this machine at the time of its sale, this machine was clearly not fit for its intended purpose, namely the washing of clothes. I therefore reach the conclusion that the plaintiff is entitled to succeed under subsection 1.

That leads to a consideration of the subsection which provides that in the case of a sale of goods by a business there is an implied condition on the part of the seller that the goods are of merchantable quality. Now there has been much written about what these words mean. In the course of argument, several quotations from various decided cases have been read to me, some of which seem far removed from the simple case of a defective washing machine.

So far as this case is concerned, I consider that the most helpful authority is Grant v Australian Knitting Mills, where Mr. Justice Dixon said: 'The condition that the goods are of merchantable quality requires that they should be in such an actual state that a buyer fully acquainted with the facts and, therefore, knowing what hidden defects exist and not being limited to their apparent condition would buy them without abatement of the price obtainable for such goods if in reasonably sound order and condition and without special terms.'

Applying that test—the hidden defect test—I have no hesitation in finding that an ordinary buyer of a washing machine, knowing what lay in store regarding this washing machine, with its prospect of breakdowns and difficulties, would not have accepted it. In those circumstances, it must follow that this machine was not, at the time of its delivery to the plaintiff's house, of merchantable quality. I find therefore that the plaintiff is entitled to succeed under subsection 2 also.

In those circumstances, the plaintiff is entitled to judgment in this case. I find that her rejection of the goods in December 1972 was reasonable and not too late. In this case it was understood on both sides that faults would be attended to under the guarantee by the manufacturers, so that a buyer who chooses to allow the manufacturers a chance to correct faults under a guarantee should not automatically lose the right to reject the goods later on, if in the course of time it becomes clear that the manufacturers cannot or will not put right those faults. When that time comes—and in this case it did not come until December—the buyer must act promptly, and must reject the goods without delay. That is what the plaintiff did in this case, and I hold it to have been a valid rejection of the goods within the requirements of the law.

I would only add that if I am wrong on that, I would hold as an alternative that the plaintiff is entitled to damages for breach of contract on account of the defects in the machine. On that hypothesis, the amount of damages she would have been entitled to would be the difference between the price she paid and the value of this washing machine. There is no direct evidence before me of the value of the machine with all its defects, but bearing in mind what I have heard about it, I cannot imagine that any householder would pay anything for it. On that basis, then, the plaintiff would be entitled by way of damages to a sum equal to the price she paid, that is £84.50. If, therefore, I had found that the plaintiff's rejection of the machine had come too late, I would have awarded by way of damages a sum equal to the price she paid.

There is also the item of special damage, amounting to £12.40. This has been agreed, so that I need spend no more time on it. This sum will be added to the award to the plaintiff.

Finally, I must deal with the question of compensation for the loss of use of the washing machine, inconvenience, misery, disappointment and trouble, and the continuing expense that the plaintiff incurred to get her washing done from the date she issued the summons in this case until the date that she bought another machine. The plaintiff is entitled to general damages for these matters. She has graphically described the frustration and inconvenience, the upset and disappointment, which she endured during the few months of her ownership of this machine. She thought she was buying a means of lightening her household burden, and a joy and a comfort in the home. She bought what I might be forgiven for describing as a load of trouble. I bear in mind that—resulting from the Court of Appeal's judgment in the case of Jarvis v Swans Tours—it is now clear that disappointment and upset are matters that can be reflected in the award of damages for breach of contract. That case also demonstrates that the amount of damages to be awarded in a case like this is not confined to the price of the appliance. In other words, it is not the law that the price of £84.50 should in some way dictate the amount of compensation to be awarded. But in any event the plaintiff has limited her claim for general damages to £100. In my view £35 would be an appropriate sum in all the circumstances to cover the matters relied on under this head of her claim for damages.

The plaintiff will have judgment for £131.90, that is £84.50, the price, plus £12.40 the agreed items of special damage, plus £35 general damages.

The plaintiff is also entitled to costs. Mrs. Seaton, as you have been a litigant in person, the amount of costs you may receive is somewhat limited. You are entitled to receive from the defendants the amount you expended, that is, your actual out of pocket expenses incurred in bringing this case. That would include the court fee on issuing the summons, a witness allowance for yourself and your two witnesses, and other actual expenditure. But that's all.'

Under the Litigants in Person (Costs and Expenses) Act 1975, a person who wins a court case without having a solicitor is entitled to receive, as part of the award of costs against the loser, payment for work done, and loss and expenses incurred, through bringing the case. The rules lay down how much can be received in an individual case, which can include something for loss of earnings involved in attending court to issue the summons and attending the pre-trial review. The act applies to steps taken in a case from 1 January 1976 onwards. But it does not apply to cases where less than £100 is at stake. There the 'no costs' rule prevents the winner getting costs, whether he has a solicitor or not. Emma's case would have been covered by the act, had it taken place in or after 1976.

The judge now continued: 'You may consider it to be an advantage if I were to assess here and now the amount to be paid to cover your costs or perhaps they may be agreed, to save having the additional trouble and expense of a taxation by the registrar, that is, a separate hearing later on, when your claim for costs is vetted, item by item. There is no need for that, do you think?'

—costs

'I will be guided by you, your honour,' said Emma. 'I would naturally welcome any means of avoiding having to come here again to deal with the costs, and if it is purely a matter of totting up my out of pocket expenses, I do not think it should be difficult. In fact, as it happens, I have already prepared—just in case I should win my case—a note of all those expenses which I have incurred, and which I think I am allowed. I typed it out, with two copies. I have it here.' Emma produced her memo setting out her expenses. This is how it was worded:

Seaton v Watsons Stores (Minford) Ltd
Plaint No 72/00534
Expenses of Mrs. Emma Seaton in connection with her case

	£ p
1. Court fees—issuing summons	5.00
witness summons	10
2. Defendant's solicitors' charge for supplying copies of documents (2 sets)	2.40
3. Copying charges for preparation of bundles of documents for the trial (2 sets)	1.90

4. Witness expenses (assuming one whole day at court):

	Allowance	*Travelling Expenses*	
(a) Self (housewife)	£4*	0.10	4.10
(b) Mr. M. J. Seaton (company secretary)	£10*	0.10	10.10
(c) Mr. D. Richardson (service mechanic)	£4*	0.50	4.50

    * Maximum sums per day allowed.

	£ p
5. Travelling expenses to issue summons (0.10), to attend pre-trial review (0.10), to issue witness summons (0.10), to serve witness summons (0.30) and to swear affidavit of service (0.10)	0.70
6. Postage, stationery, phone calls, purchase of *How to sue in the county court*	3.50
Total	£32.30

She handed one copy to the judge and another to counsel for Watsons. Both looked at it with care.

'Do you have any comments on any of these items, Mr. Sanders?' asked the judge. Counsel pondered.

'The plaintiffs husband is, I accept, a professional man, but I suggest that he ought not to receive the maximum of £10 a day, bearing in mind that he gave evidence, not as a professional witness, but in his private capacity as the plaintiff's husband. Secondly, I find difficulty in accepting the last item, your honour. I observe it includes the price of a book.'

'Perhaps, I should explain,' said Emma rising to her feet 'that without this very book I could not have brought this case, and certainly not pursued it as far as I have.'

'I will allow it as an item, and I think £6 for Mr. Seaton's witness allowance. The other items on your list I will allow as claimed. I therefore assess the costs in the sum of £28.30. There is presumably no question of your client asking for time to pay, Mr. Sanders?'

'None, your honour.'

'Very well, then, that will be the order I make.' The judge smiled at Emma and at Mr. Sanders, collected his papers, and rose to his feet. Everyone in the court did likewise and he left the court.

If you organise events so that, in order to settle a dispute, you are the one to be sued rather the one who sues, you are much better placed. Suing in the county court is a risk, an expense, a nerve-racking, time consuming experience. If, therefore, you can effectively put the boot on to the other foot, and make a shop, or other trader, have to take the initiative in bringing a case against you in the county court, if it wants to prove its point, this is the better thing to do.

Take a simple case: you order something in a shop, charge the cost to your account there. Soon after, you discover a fault. You can recoup the cost of repairing the fault out of the money you have in hand for the price. If the goods are so faulty that they are not fit for their intended purpose—if they don't work, in fact—you can cancel the purchase altogether, and require the seller to take the goods back. You need not pay the price when this happens, and you have a complete defence if the seller brings a court case against you for payment of the price. If the fault is a small one, so that a little expense in repairing it would be all that is necessary, you could deduct the expense, setting it off against the price. In practice, this would only arise where the seller refuses to do anything about putting right the fault himself. It is always wise—although not legally necessary—to ask the shop to do something about a fault, before invoking your legal rights in the matter.

If you are buying goods on hire purchase or any other form of credit, the position gets a bit more complicated. In the case of a hire purchase deal, irrespective whether the goods are new or secondhand, the finance company—the firm with whom you have the agreement to pay so much a week or month—is responsible for any faults. You can therefore deduct the cost of putting right faults, plus any incidental expenses, from future instalments due under the hire purchase agreement. This is an important consumer right, and one which is largely ignored in practice. Legally it is perfectly valid.

If the finance company want to contest your right to do this, they have to take you to court. They have to sue you for the current instalments due under the hire purchase agreement. If they do, you should defend the case, relying on your right to set off your claim against theirs. You say, in effect, that the hire purchase instalments have been paid by you—they have been settled by a process of subtraction, a process of set-off, so that they are no longer due to the finance company. This is not the same thing as saying that, because the article was faulty, you are not obliged to keep up the instalments. That is not so. The position is that the finance company must pay for putting right faults, including consequential expenses such as hire charges, and that your liability to pay the instalments is met by deducting your claim from the instalments due.

The right to recoup the cost of hiring a replacement used to apply only when the article you bought was a new one, because there your rights could not be diminished by any small print in the hire purchase agreement. Until 1973, this was not the case with a secondhand car, or anything else secondhand.

Even though you cannot expect secondhand goods to be as good as new ones, your rights regarding them when buying them on hire purchase are now to the same general effect. So if you buy on hire purchase a secondhand car which needs substantial repairs soon after you get it, you have the right to deduct the cost of the repair from the debt.

But you still do not have the right to deduct from instalments where you are buying with a personal loan, because in that case the moneylending operation is quite separate from the purchase of the car, or other article. The rights you have about defects lie against the garage or shop which sold the article, and the finance company or bank which made the personal loan does not come into it.

Because of the difficulties and expense generally thought to be involved in taking a claim to the county court, you may find that your opponent does not bother, and just lets the matter drop. If so, you have, in effect, won the point, and with a whole lot less trouble than if the matter had gone to court. But not until six years have passed are you immune from liability to pay a debt.

You may find that the matter is passed to solicitors or debt collectors. If this happens, they may ignore your protestation that you are not liable to pay what is claimed. The other side may treat your case just as if you were not paying a debt. It can be very annoying to receive a standard debt collection letter from a solicitor or a debt collection agency, when all the time—as the firm you are dealing with should know—you have been contesting their right to have the money. If this happens, you are justified in writing a firm letter in reply, referring to previous correspondence and discussions on the matter in dispute.

If the worst comes to the worst, and the matter ends in court, you will be the defendant, and the person claiming from you will be the plaintiff. The procedure in this situation is the mirror image of what happened when Emma Seaton claimed from Watsons for damages regarding her defective washing machine. The procedure when you are a defendant is much the same as when you are a plaintiff, but now you generally find it is up to the other side to take the initiative at each stage. Your role is to respond in each instance.

the summons
The first formal step when you are being sued is that you are served with the summons. A court official, the bailiff, may come to your house, and hand the summons to you. Alternatively, the summons may be sent through the post. There are usually three distinct forms that come. The first is the summons itself, which tells you that you are summoned to appear as the defendant in a case in the particular county court. In the case of an ordinary summons, it tells you when the hearing of the pre-trial review will take place. If, however, the plaintiff has issued a default summons, there is no date mentioned for any hearing. In either case you have to respond with your defence within 14 days, and that is what the summons tells you. The second form that comes (form 18A) is the one on which you can, if you like, write your defence. It also

provides a place for you to counterclaim or to admit the claim (if you do) and to offer payment by instalments or to ask for the case to be referred to arbitration. If you intend to contest the case, you do not need to use this form at all, but can prepare your defence on a separate piece of paper. The third document you receive is probably the most important one. This is called the particulars of claim, and it sets out exactly what the plaintiff is claiming. Lawyers tend to draft particulars of claim with a good deal of legal jargon, and it may not be easy to understand what they are saying. You have to do the best you can.

If the summons has been issued in a county court which is not your local one, you are entitled to ask for the case to be transferred. All you need to do is write a letter to the registrar of the court where the summons was issued, asking that the case be transferred to your local county court. He will consider the request on its merit and there is a good chance that he will transfer it, particularly if the other court is far away from where you live.

the defence

You have to set out the details of why you say you need not pay. You can do this either on form 18A which has been sent to you (continuing on to a fresh sheet of paper if you run out of space on the form), or you can write the whole defence on a separate piece of paper. If you use your own piece of paper for your defence, you should follow the layout that the plaintiff's solicitors adopted in preparing the particulars of claim. You start with the action heading, that is, the name of the particular county court, the plaint number, followed by the name of the plaintiff and your name, as the defendant. (On form 18A these details have to be completed.) Then you write 'Defence' as a heading. Now comes the text of the defence, in which you set out in paragraphs the details of what you say is the basis for your not paying what is claimed. You may start, for instance, by admitting certain parts of the particulars of claim. There is often no dispute about the basic facts of the matter; that you had a contract with the plaintiff, say, under which he was to supply you with certain goods, or to perform certain services. Admit facts which you feel are not in dispute. Indeed, if you do not when it would be reasonable for you to do so, you may find that, although you win the case in the end, you may be penalised for the amount of any costs involved in proving facts which could have been admitted.

There are likely to be certain parts of the particulars of claim which you do not admit. In this case, your defence will say something like this: 'Paragraphs 1 to 5 inclusive of the particulars of claim are admitted. Paragraphs 6 to 9 inclusive are denied.'

There may be some facts which you are not quite sure about. In other words, you may feel that something which the plaintiff alleges, in his particulars of claim is probably true—but you cannot be sure. In this situation, you are quite entitled to call on him to prove it, if he can. In this case you say in your defence: 'Paragraph 5 of the particulars of claim is not admitted.'

It may be that you can admit the whole of the particulars of claim but that you have a counterclaim. In this case your defence should be headed 'Defence and Counterclaim' and your first paragraph would say 'I admit the plaintiff's claim'. Then you would go on to say: 'I have a counterclaim against the plaintiff which arises in the following way.' (Form 18A has a space for this.) You then set out the basis of your counterclaim in the same way as you would have done, if you had been claiming in a case you yourself had brought. In other words, your defence and counter-claim then proceed like a particulars of claim, and is set out in a similar way. It might end up something like this: 'I therefore claim £. . . . from the plaintiff. This is equal to (or more than) the amount of the plaintiff's claim against me, which I have admitted. I am therefore not liable to pay the amount claimed by the plaintiff.' If the amount of your counterclaim is for more than the amount of the plaintiff's claim against you, you would end by claiming the extra. If you were to do this, you may have to pay a court fee on the amount of the balance you were claiming. This is because you are, in effect, starting a court case against the plaintiff for this balance.

If you want the case to be referred to arbitration, say so at the end of your defence. If more than £100 is claimed, the case can only go to arbitration if both sides agree. The registrar will decide about this at the pre-trial review.

Keep a copy of your defence for your own file.

further and better particulars
You may find that the particulars of claim does not

contain enough detail for you to understand fully what the plaintiff is getting at. Or there may be some confusion in the way the plaintiff states his claim, so that it does not make sense to you. If this happens, you are entitled to ask the plaintiff's solicitors for 'further and better particulars' of the claim. You might say something like this: 'I have received the particulars of claim in this case, and have been studying it with care. There are one or two points which are not clear to me, and I would be grateful therefore if you would let me have further details of the following: In paragraph 3: please state the date when, according to the plaintiff, I agreed to have an alternative structure for the roof of the extension, and state where this discussion took place, and who else was present. If any reference to this modification in the original order appears in any of the documents, please say which one. In paragraph 7: please state the basis on which it is claimed that labour charges amounting to £74.90 were incurred for the extra items, giving the number of hours worked by each man involved, the rate of pay, the number of men who worked, and the dates on which the work involved was carried out.

I look forward to hearing from you.'

If the plaintiff's solicitors refuse to provide information which you feel is necessary in order for you to know all about the case, you can raise it with the registrar. This could be done at the pre-trial review. As a rule, you will be able to frame your defence without getting the further particulars, so you should go ahead with preparing and delivering your defence, at the same time asking for the further particulars. If you do not get them, state that you will raise the question at the pre-trial review.

The plaintiff's solicitors may want you to provide further particulars of your defence. They would normally ask for this in a letter, but they may send a formal request for further and better particulars. In any event, you could provide the details in a letter. You might refuse them, if you felt they were not entitled to them and again the question could be resolved by the registrar at the pre-trial review.

payment into court

If you admit part but not all of the plaintiff's claim, you should pay into court the amount which you admit. This you should do as soon as possible. Take an example: imagine that you are in dispute with a garage about servicing and repairs to your car. They have sent you a bill which you think is too high, as it includes items for some work which you think was unnecessary, and which you did not ask to have done. After a rather unsatisfactory exchange of correspondence, they issue a summons in the county court for the full amount of their bill. To save you legal costs it is important that you should—as soon as you can—work out the amount which you agree is due to them, and pay this sum into court without delay.

If you admit part of the plaintiff's claim, but not all, you would say in your defence something like this: 'I admit £   of the plaintiff's claim, but no more', proceeding then to explain why you consider the claim to be excessive. To pay a sum into court you should write to the registrar of the court explaining the situation, and enclosing a postal order or money order for the amount you wish to pay, made out to 'The Paymaster General'.

If the plaintiff wishes to dispute matters raised by you in your defence, he may prepare a document called a reply, which will be sent to you. The reply sets out the plaintiff's response to questions of fact raised in the defence which he disputes, and which affect the outcome of his claim. The plaintiff may put in a defence to a counterclaim.

procedure
The procedure in a disputed county court case is broadly the same whether you are the defendant or the plaintiff. At the pre-trial review the registrar may help with any difficulties or uncertainties that may have arisen regarding the defence. He may be able to suggest ways of narrowing the differences between the plaintiff and yourself, or refer the case to arbitration. He may, however, consider that your defence does not reveal a legal basis for resisting the plaintiff's claim. He may therefore suggest that you would be better advised to abandon your defence, and consent to judgment against you. You may be wise to do as he suggests. You are, however, quite entitled to stand your ground and fight on.

It is always worth while trying to compromise before the trial, if at all possible. You can negotiate with the plaintiff's solicitors and extract the best bargain you can.

If it was an ordinary summons that you received, it

is less important that you should lodge your defence in court within 14 days. In fact, even if you do nothing before attending the hearing of the pre-trial review, you would then be allowed to put in your defence, and the case would proceed as if you had put in your defence at the right time. The registrar usually stipulates how much longer you are to have before the defence must be put in. If you do not comply with that, the plaintiff could get judgment against you, because of your failure to put in your defence. All the same, it is best to put in your defence in time, if you can.

In the case of a default summons, however, it is important that you should put in your defence in time, that is, within 14 days of the time when the summons was served on you. After you have put in your defence, you may then receive a form stating a day—often about a month ahead—when the pre-trial review will be heard. If you do not put your defence in within the 14 days, the chances are that the plaintiff will then apply for a judgment against you by reason of your default without a hearing.

If you were to ignore a default summons until it was too late, all would not be lost, however. Even though the plaintiff has obtained judgment against you on his claim, by reason of your failure to respond to the summons within the time allowed, you could still apply to the court to set aside the judgment, and to be allowed to defend the case after all. If you were to do this it is quite likely that the judgment would be set aside. There would then be a hearing at which you would be allowed to defend. But you would probably be ordered (win or lose) to pay the legal costs incurred by the plaintiff as a result of the case being set aside, as these costs were incurred because of your failure to respond to the summons in time.

Between the pre-trial review and the hearing of the case, you would proceed to prepare your case in much the same way as a plaintiff would. If there were quite a few documents on each side connected with the case, the registrar may order discovery of documents. It would be wise to interview any witnesses you proposed to call, and—if possible—get statements from them, so that you knew what they would be likely to say on the day. If someone was unwilling to come to court to be a witness, you would have to apply to the court office for a witness summons, and serve it or have it served on the person concerned. If you wanted the witness to bring to court any documents, or other items of evidence to help prove your case, the witness summons would have to provide for this.

settling

To be sued is in some ways almost as hazardous as it is to sue. You may start resisting a claim, full of bravado and determination. After a time, your enthusiasm may wane, and you may feel inclined to abandon your defence. Your instincts are probably right about this. It is always better to settle a case, if you can. The outcome, once battle is joined, is nearly always a matter of some uncertainty, and this uncertainty may wear you down as much as the prospect of being severely out of pocket as a result of losing.

Only the most determined should pursue a defence, and then only in cases which have legal merit. If these conditions are fulfilled, however, your determination may be enough to induce your adversary to lose heart. Only a tiny minority of cases actually come to a hearing. If you know how to fight a claim against you, if you have to, the chances are that you will not have to. The important thing is not to abandon the idea of fighting a case, just because you do not think it is worth while to employ a solicitor.

The decision of the judge or registrar in a case is embodied in a document, which is sent to the loser within a few days of the hearing. It is called the judgment and states the amount the loser has to pay to the winner, and the time by which payment has to be made—this is fourteen days from the date of the judgment unless something different was ordered.

appeal

The loser in a court case sometimes wants to appeal against the decision. For cases where £20 or less is claimed there is no appeal from the decision of a judge, unless the judge gives special permission. But the person who loses a county court case where more than £20 was at stake, can appeal as of right. Where a case was tried by a judge, the appeal is made to the Court of Appeal, a very lofty tribunal, part of the Supreme Court of Judicature, which sits in London.

When the amount at stake was between £20 and £200, the appeal can be made only on a point of law, and not on a point of fact. In a case, for instance, where the judge had to decide the exact legal meaning of the words 'merchantable quality' the result of his interpretation might well decide in whose favour he gave judgment. His decision as to what the law really meant was a decision on a point of law, and so could have formed the basis of an appeal to the Court of Appeal.

Before the judge got as far as deciding what the law was, he had to make various findings of fact, that is to decide what happened. There is no appeal to the Court of Appeal from a county court judge's finding of fact, unless the amount in dispute is over £200.

The procedure for appealing is quite complicated. Notice of appeal has to be given within six weeks of the date of the judge's decision. So the winner cannot be sure that he will not be faced with an appeal by the loser until six weeks have passed.

In county court cases decided by the registrar— generally those where the amount at stake is not more than £100—either side can ask to appeal to the judge from the decision of the registrar. This can be on a question of law or on a question of fact, and applies not only to his final decision on the trial of a case, but to any decision of his on any other matter. To enter an appeal, you have to complete a form (form 25) obtainable from the court office.

Following an arbitration, however, an appeal can be only on a point of law.

taxation of costs

Unless the costs were assessed at the trial, they are worked out in detail by a procedure called taxation. For this, a hearing takes place before the registrar some time after the completion of the trial. He goes through the winner's itemised bill of costs and decides what items are to be allowed and the amount for each item. Each item repesents a piece of work needed to carry the case forward to the next stage. Expenses—such as court fees, witness allowances and travelling expenses—are listed, too. The winner's solicitor must prepare his bill according to a set pattern, using the appropriate scale as the basis of how much to claim in every instance.

There are, in effect, five scales: the 'lower scale' and scales 1, 2, 3 and 4. Which scale applies in any individual case depends on the amount at stake in the case, and is determined by the judge at the trial. Generally, the following applies: up to £20 at stake, 'lower scale'; over £20 and up to £50, scale 1; over £50 and up to £200, scale 2; over £200 and up to £500, scale 3; over £500, scale 4. The higher the scale, the higher the amount of costs payable.

Naturally, the winner wants to recover as much as possible by way of costs. Similarly, the loser wants to have to pay as little as possible. He wants to argue that less than the maximum should be allowed for each item and that some of the items in the winner's bill of costs should not be allowed at all, on the grounds that they were not necessary to get the case ready for trial. The purpose of taxation is to decide arguments of this kind.

Usually, a bill of costs is prepared for taxation by a firm of solicitors and its main ingredients are items for solicitors' fees. If the winner did not employ a solicitor to fight his case, his bill for taxation would consist of his out-of-pocket expenses only, such as court fees, postage, stationery, fares and witnesses' expenses. From 1976, he can claim payment for the work involved as well.

enforcing a judgment

One of the most important functions of the county court is to see that debts are paid. Indeed, many more cases are brought in the county court for the purpose of pursuing debtors than are ever brought for the purpose of resolving disputes. But if a man simply does not have the means to pay, and no prospects of getting such means, a judgment is useless, and the legal costs expended in procuring the judgment will be good money thrown after bad.

There have been cases of door-to-door salesmen for such things as central heating systems, freezers and double glazing units who have taken people in, and relieved them of deposits without producing anything to show for it. After a delay during which nothing has happened, the unfortunate customer may start making enquiries, only to find that the firm is out of business, or a liquidator has been appointed. In this situation, the customer is in much the same position as a finance company pursuing a feckless debtor. In other words he ought to consider carefully first whether it is worth suing. If the firm has gone out of business without any assets and there is really no prospect of recovering anything, you should abandon the matter. If there does seem to be a slim prospect of recovering something from a crumbling firm, it is usually important to act quickly. The sooner you start a court case, the greater the chance that you will get something.

When the county court performs its role of providing a means of resolving disputes about legal liability, there is often no problem about enforcing the decision of the court, once it is given. The victorious consumer in a county court case will probably not run into trouble in getting his money where his erstwhile opponent is a shop, a garage, an insurance company, or some kind of business which is still operating.

Occasionally you may find that even after a dispute

with a shop, or some apparently flourishing business, you have difficulty in getting your money, after the court has given a judgment in your favour. It may happen, for instance, that a shop is so angry at having lost the case that it simply will not pay, merely out of pique. Or a business may be so disorganised that it just does not pay up, even though the court has ordered it to do so. Some firms are so bureaucratic thay they have (they say) no means of paying money out unless they have an invoice. In situations like this, you can seriously consider using any of the means available by law to enforce your judgment.

If a county court judgment for £10 or more (including in that sum any costs owing) is not paid for a month or more after the date of judgment, particulars of it are entered on the register of county court judgments. The registry is kept by the Registrar of County Court Judgments, 140 Gower Street, London, WC1E 6HT, where anyone may search to find out whether any judgments are registered against a particular name. It costs 10p to make a search if you visit there personally. It is 25p, if done by post. It costs more if you want to go back more than three years. Finance companies, banks and other providers of credit refer to this defaulters' register constantly. So ending up on the register of judgments is a big black mark in one's credit rating.

It is a matter of automatic routine for the debtor's name to go on the register, once a judgment for £10 or more has been entered, a month has gone by since the date of the judgment and the debt has not been reduced to less than £10. For this reason, it is as well

for the debtor to try and reduce the amount to below
£10 as soon as he can, and at any rate before the
month is up, if this is at all possible. Likewise, if he
makes any payments to reduce what is owing, he will
be wise to make sure they go to the court to which he
was ordered to pay, and not direct to the person to
whom they are due. Otherwise, he may find that the
court has no knowledge of the debt being reduced
below £10, or having been paid off entirely perhaps,
and his name will have been entered on the register
when it would not have been if he had obeyed the
order to pay into court.

When a judgment is finally paid off, it is not automatically removed from the register. The debtor has
to apply for the debt to be deregistered; the fee is
10p.

—execution

The court will not attempt to enforce a judgment
unless formally requested. Enforcement of a judgment
debt by execution consists of obtaining a warrant
from the court, followed by the court bailiff entering
the premises of the debtor and seizing goods that
belong to the debtor. The chances are—if the debtor
has any money—that he will immediately pay the
debt and the costs, rather than lose his goods. If he
does not pay, the bailiff takes possession of the
goods. They can then be sold by auction and the debt
and the costs can be paid out of the proceeds of the
sale. Things on hire purchase cannot be seized, as
they still belong to the finance company. It may be
claimed that the furniture belongs, say, to the debtor's

wife, in which case evidence in writing to support such a claim will be required by the bailiff.

The snag about execution is the extra cost it involves. The victorious plaintiff has to pay further court fees in order to obtain a warrant of execution. Where the judgment is for £80 or less, the fee is 25p for every £2, or part of £2. So, on a judgment where, say, £38 for the debt and costs is owing, the court fee for obtaining the warrant would be £4.25. On £80 the fee would be £10. This is in fact the maximum, so it would be the same in the case of a judgment for, say, £500. To put £10 at risk on the off-chance that the debtor has assets sufficient to meet the total due may not be wise. The auction of goods seized in execution seldom raises much money, and the cost of removal and sale, which has to come out of them, is high. Execution is often a precarious remedy from the creditor's point of view.

—garnishee proceedings

Perhaps the next most likely means of enforcing a judgment debt is called garnishee proceedings. This is really only any good if you know the bank and the branch, where the shop (or whoever else your debtor is) has an account—as a result of having in the past received a cheque from them, for instance.

This is the procedure: you apply in the county court for the district covering the branch in question. (If this is not the same county court as the one where you have obtained the judgment, you must obtain a certificate of the judgment from the court which gave it. The fee is 5p.) You attend at the court office, taking the plaint note, and ask them for form 205, the affidavit (i.e. sworn statement) you have to provide about the judgment debt and the bank account. You have to swear (in effect) that you have good reason to believe that the judgment debtor has a bank account at the stated bank and branch and that it is in credit. The court fee to be paid on applying for a garnishee order is £5, where the amount involved is £100 or more; under that, it is 5p for every £1 or part. A hearing date is fixed by the court and the garnishee summons is served on the bank, both at its registered office and at the branch in question. If the debtor's account is in credit, the bank will then pay into court the amount on the garnishee summons, or the whole amount of its customer's credit balance if this is less. You are notified and have to write to the court and to the bank, accepting the amount paid into court. The bank is then finished with the proceedings. If you can get the debtor's consent in writing, the court will then pay you out. If not, you have to attend the hearing of the garnishee summons, ask for an order for payment out, and will then receive the money.

—attachment of earnings

In the case of a judgment against an individual, it is sometimes possible to obtain the money by getting a court order for the sum to be paid out of his wages or salary, by instalments. This is called attachment of earnings. You must apply in the court for the district where the debtor currently resides. He is served with a summons (which costs up to £10 to issue), and within 14 days of receiving this summons, the debtor has to provide particulars of his income and expenditure each week or month, and the name and address of his employer. The court can require the employer to give particulars of the debtor's earnings. There is then a hearing in chambers (that is, in private) when the registrar decides how much the debtor needs to live on, and how much, in the circumstances, he should have deducted each week or each month out of his pay, to go towards reducing what he owes. It is unwise to apply unless you are sure he is in stable employment (not self-employed) and unlikely suddenly to change his job, and not already financially over-committed.

—*other means of enforcement*

It is possible to make a person officially bankrupt, if he owes at least £50. When this happens—and the process is complicated—the whole of his financial affairs are taken out of his hands, and his assets are realised for the benefit of all his creditors. In the case of a limited company, the equivalent process is called liquidation; the winding up of the affairs of the company is then in the hands of the liquidator.

Another process available sometimes is the appointment of a receiver, that is, someone (usually an accountant) who will receive monies due to the debtor as they come in; rents, perhaps, or dividends from shares. The receiver pays his own fees first out of what he gets, and hands the rest over in order to pay what is due on the judgment debt.

If the debtor owns a property, such as a house, you can obtain from the court a charging order on the property. This acts someting like a mortgage on the house. The result would be that the house could not be sold without the debt being paid, and in certain cases a sale could be forced, to obtain what is due.

Enforcement of a debt by legal process is a complicated and expensive business, can be frustrated by a debtor who knows the ropes, and in any case cannot produce money where there is none to be had. This consideration also applies to any court claim you may contemplate bringing: do not sue unless there is a reasonable prospect of your being paid at the end.

If you have used this book to bring a case in the county court, please let us know how you got on.

INDEX

Abandoning, 92, 225
affidavit, 103, 150, 236
– of service,. 111, 148, 149
appeal, 229 *et seq*
arbitration, 26, 29, 32, 53, 98, 153, 220, 222, 225, 230
assignee, 57
attachment of earnings, 236

bank account, 235, 236
bankrupt, 237
barrister, 24, 33, 85, 105, 124, 155 (*see also* counsel)
breakdown, 10, 12, 15, 45, 82, 169, 176, 186, 205, 206

cancelling a purchase, 5, 11, 12, 18, 21, 22, 164, 171, 216
– in time, 14, 15, 203, 210
chambers, in, 34, 52, 95, 153, 237
Companies' House, 38, 39
company's name, 38, 39, 40
compensation, 5, 11, 14, 15, 36, 51, 63, 211

conduct money, 112, 140
contemporaneous notes, 128, 167, 185
contract, 4, 5, 37, 50, 208
– breach of, 6, 13, 45, 55, 61, 206, 211
– cancelling, 13
corroboration, 183
costs, 8, 9, 24, 45, 47, 53, 66, 68, 69, 92, 98, 99, 212, 213, 214, 227, 230
– fixed, 25
– taxed, 26, 230
counsel, 24, 33, 105, 171, 188
counterclaim, 220, 222, 225
county court, 8, 9, 24, 28, 32, 35, 37, 54, 98, 218, 232
– district, 1, 37, 54, 55, 60, 220, 235
court fees, 27, 52, 61, 62, 230, 235, 236
court order, 28
cross-examination, 2, 33, 171 *et seq*, 188, 197

damages, 1, 5, 7, 14, 36, 45, 49, 51, 211
– general, 51, 52, 212

– special, 51, 101, 102, 211, 212

debt, 5, 6, 28, 35, 51, 57, 218, 231, 234

default, 32

defects, 5, 10, 12, 13, 20, 21, 77, 160, 164, 166, 208

– hidden, 210

defence, 7, 30, 53, 72, 78, 82 *et seq,* 96, 190, 220, 226

defendant, 30, 32, 37, 47, 48, 53, 58, 84, 190, 219

discovery, 89, 90, 102

documents, 24, 73, 83, 98, 102, 104, 106, 113, 114, 117, 122, 123, 129, 143, 162

– copying of, 126, 130

– discovery of, 31, 89, 113, 227

– inspection of, 119, 125, 126, 128, 138

– priveleged, 114, 115, 124

enforcement, 8, 28, 231, 234, 237,

evidence, 2, 13, 17, 31, 78, 81, 86, 87, 88, 98, 100, 167

– agreed, 99, 151, 162, 201

– in chief, 166

examination-in-chief, 166

execution, 234

expenses, 5, 10, 13, 15, 24, 27, 45, 46, 49, 101, 111, 231

expert, 76, 78, 98, 99, 208

– inspection, 100, 127, 150

final address, 201, 203

further particulars, 71, 75, 81, 88, 222

garnishee proceedings, 235

guarantee, 3, 10, 12, 19, 163, 196, 197, 205, 208

hearsay, 169

hire purchase, 6, 11, 216, 234

injunction, 50

inspection of documents, 119, 125, 126, 128, 129, 138

judge, 1, 26, 29, 33, 155, 159, 203, 205, 229

judgment, 8, 32, 53, 98, 205, 210, 225, 226, 229, 233

lawyers' fees, 24, 25, 26, 63
leading question, 181
legal expenses, 8
legal rights, 2, 4, 6, 7, 22, 165
limited company, 37, 38, 39, 40, 63
liquidated sum, 36, 53
litigant in person's costs, 63, 213, 231
loser, 8, 24, 53, 108, 229

man of straw, 8
manufacturer, 3, 10, 11, 12, 17, 20, 23, 164, 196, 205, 208
minor, 57, 59

notice to admit, 133, 135
notice to produce, 133, 134

offer of settlement, 17
official order, 106, 107
Oyez shop, 112, 113, 133

particulars of claim, 30, 35, 41 *et seq,* 53, 73, 84, 96, 106, 220
payment into court, 67, 69, 224, 234, 236
personal loan, 218
plaint fee, 62, 63, 212
plaint note, 64, 65, 93, 108, 236
plaint number, 48, 64, 108, 221
plaintiff, 30, 32, 45, 47, 48, 53, 56, 84, 203, 219
– 's opening, 160
pleadings, 31, 89, 97
praecipe, 56, 108
pre-trial review, 31, 32, 34, 65, 79, 93 *et seq,* 222, 225
procedure, 2, 7, 22, 30, 32, 34, 54, 225
– simple, 29, 30, 98
proprietor's name, 39, 40
publicity, 66, 152

re-examination, 183, 190
referee, 98, 99
refunding of price, 12, 15, 18, 19, 22, 45, 46, 52, 161, 162
register of county court judgments, 233
registered office, 21, 35, 37, 38, 53, 58, 60

registrar, 29, 32, 95, 98, 99, 222, 229, 230
– 's room, 34, 94
reply, 225
request, 35, 54, 55, 56, 108
road accident, 4, 5, 36

Sale of Goods Act 1893, 4, 5, 13, 20, 21, 44, 46, 49, 67, 161, 191, 192, 193, 202, 206, 209
secondhand, 217, 218
settlement, 32, 66, 68, 70, 156, 227
– out of court, 66
shop, 2, 3, 4, 7, 11, 16, 19, 23, 27, 199, 233
small claims, 26, 29, 53, 98
solicitor, 8, 16, 21, 22, 71, 124, 139
– without, 3, 4, 5, 7, 30, 33, 63, 97, 152, 158, 213, 231
summons, 22, 25, 26, 35, 36, 40, 47, 53, 54, 64, 219, 236
– default, 35, 53, 54, 219, 226
– ordinary, 35, 36, 54, 55, 56, 219, 225
– by post, 64, 219

swearing, 101, 103, 149, 150, 166, 236

taking back goods, 14, 20
taxation, 26, 230
time limit, 18, 23, 204, 205
trial, 26, 31, 34, 97, 157 *et seq,* 230

warrant, 234
washing machine, 10, 12, 16, 18, 19, 21, 36, 45, 74, 80, 82, 100, 123, 127, 150, 161, 165, 169, 195
winner, 8, 25, 66, 229
without prejudice, 17, 69, 156
witness, 2, 24, 88, 98, 101, 108, 128, 180, 215
– box, 110, 159, 166, 184
– for defence, 194
– documents, 108, 120, 140, 142
– statement, 111, 122, 139, 145, 227
– summons, 101, 108, 111, 119, 121, 138, 141, 150, 227

The legal side of buying a house

explains the legal processes of buying an owner-occupied house with a registered title in England and Wales (not Scotland) and describes the part played by the solicitors and building society, the estate agent, surveyor, Land Registry, insurance company and local authority. It takes you step by step through a typical purchase and also deals with the legal side of selling a house.

Wills and probate

is a book about wills and how to make them and about the administration of an estate by executors without the help of a solicitor. It shows, with examples, how to prepare a will, sign it, and have it witnessed. A special section deals with intestacy.

Getting a divorce

gives a step-by-step account of the procedure for getting a divorce in England or Wales (not Scotland). It explains the grounds on which a divorce can be granted, and what has to happen before the hearing of the case in court, and afterwards, including provision for maintenance, property and children. It is written for the two people getting divorced rather than the lawyers who may act for them.

What to do when someone dies

deals with the procedures that follow a death. It covers such formalities as doctors' certificates; reporting a death to the coroner and what this entails; registration of a death and the various certificates involved. Burial and cremation are discussed and the arrangements necessary for a funeral. A final section deals with national insurance benefits that can be claimed by dependants.

Coping with disablement
is written for someone who has become disabled by illness or increasing age and who needs help and advice about how to manage everyday activities such as bathing, going to the lavatory, cooking and eating, walking, dressing. It explains about choosing a wheelchair and using it, suggests some suitable pastimes and outdoor activities, and explains where help and information can be sought—from the local authority, the national health service, voluntary organisations.

Central heating
discusses the factors to consider when you have central heating installed: from choosing the fuel and the right type and amount of insulation, to finding a good installer. The book describes, explains and illustrates the various types of boiler, radiators, convectors, circulation systems and methods of control. It gives advice on avoiding hazards and on dealing with problems after the installation.

Extending your house
tells in detail what has to be done at the various stages of a house extension scheme. It is not a do-it-yourself manual but describes the role of the architect or other consultant and the builder, and explains about planning permission and the building regulations in England and Wales. There is a glossary and many explanatory drawings.

Claiming on home, car and holiday insurance
explains the procedure for making a claim on an insurance policy, interpreting the technical jargon and identifying the people and problems you may come across.

Owning a car
for the ignorant car owner/driver, this book explains in
non-technical language what is involved in buying a car
(new or used), the responsibilities of ownership, including
repairs and maintenance, and suggests action even the most
uninitiated motorist can take if his car breaks down.

Having an operation
describes the procedure for admission to hospital and tells
you what happens there: ward routine, hospital personnel,
preparation for the operation, anaesthesia, post-operative
treatment and recovery, arrangements for discharge, and
convalescence. Basic information is given about some of
the more common operations.

Arrangements for old age
explains the functions of the services and organisations
which exist to help older people; gives advice on
occupation in retirement; explains the financial position
with regard to income tax and retirement; tells you how
to claim your retirement pension, and discusses the
problem of housing—living in your own home, with
relatives, or in a residential home.

Health for old age
sets out in plain language the minor and major physical
changes that arise as people grow older, and the treatments
available to relieve them. Advice is given about maintaining good general health, and about going to the doctor.

Infertility
sets out what can and should happen in the systematic investigation of childlessness. It will not provide a ready answer to a couple's infertility, but it puts into perspective the physical factors associated with infertility (psychological factors can only be dealt with on a person-to-person level), and explains the medical and surgical treatment at present available.

Pregnancy month by month
goes step by step through what should happen when having a baby. Some of the things that can go wrong during pregnancy and childbirth are discussed, and what can be done about them.

How to adopt
describes the process of adoption step by step. Aspects discussed in detail are eligibility to adopt, how to find a child, fostering, the child and his background, the legal situation, the effect of the adoption order—and after.

The newborn baby
discusses health and welfare in the first few weeks after the baby is born, and also deals with feeding and development in the following months. Advice is given about seeking help from midwife, health visitor, clinic doctor or general practitioner.

Caring for teeth
tells people how to look after their teeth. There is advice about diet and oral hygiene, the general dental service, private dentistry and ancillary help, dental and periodontal diseases and the treatment available, false teeth and how to look after them, and what to do and where to go in an emergency.

Treatment and care in mental illness
deals briefly with the illnesses concerned and describes the
help available from all sources. It explains the medical
treatment a mentally ill person receives as an outpatient or
an inpatient, and deals with community care and aftercare.

Eyes right
explains how the eyes work, and describes the various eye
diseases and complaints, the treatment available, including
operations on the eye. National health service and private
practice are discussed.

Electricity supply and safety
a book to help the layman understand the electrical
installations and appliances in his home. It points out the
dangers of bad wiring, amateur repairs, overloading and
faulty equipment. There are sections dealing with the
buying and using of electrical appliances, with paying, and
with the consumer's relationship to his electricity board.
Throughout, the safety aspects are stressed.

Care of the feet
discusses the structure and growth of the feet and how to look
after them, including choosing suitable shoes. Various foot
troubles and deformities are explained, and the treatments
available from doctor or chiropodist to relieve them.

Avoiding back trouble
advises on ways of avoiding back trouble and, for those who
suffer from backache and sciatic pain already, offers some
guidance on how to ease it. It explains some of the causes of
back trouble and methods of treatment; the main task,
however, is to tackle prevention.

CONSUMER PUBLICATIONS are available from
**Consumer's Association, Caxton Hill, Hertford, and from
booksellers.**